EX LIBRIS

UNIVERSITATIS SANCTI JOANNIS

Understanding
Neighborhood
Change

Understanding Neighborhood Change

The Role of Expectations in Urban Revitalization

Rolf Goetze
Research Department
Boston Redevelopment Authority

Ballinger Publishing Company • Cambridge, Massachusetts
A Subsidiary of Harper & Row, Publishers, Inc.

This book is printed on recycled paper.

Copyright © 1979 by Ballinger Publishing Company. All rights reserved. No part of this publication may be reproduced, stored in a retrieval system, or transmitted in any form or by any means, electronic, mechanical, photocopy, recording or otherwise, without the prior written consent of the publisher.

International Standard Book Number: 0−88410−493−1

Library of Congress Catalog Card Number: 79−2539

Printed in the United States of America

Library of Congress Cataloging in Publication Data

Goetze, Rolf.
  Understanding neighborhood change.

  1. Neighborhood. 2. Social change. 3. Housing—United States. 4. Residential mobility—United States. I. Title.
HT123.G572   301.5'4   79−2539
ISBN 0−88410−493−1

Contents

List of Figures

List of Tables

List of Maps

Foreword

Rolf Goetze writes in Boston but it's in Washington that people might like to ban this book. He ventures onto the *terra incognito* of neighborhood dynamics at a time when definitions, values, and economic realities affecting housing and other elements of neighborhood life are changing rapidly. His one sure conclusion is that outside interventions, however well intentioned, can have devastating effects on any neighborhood's homeostasis—its internal system of checks and balances and the social norms that lead to stability. Chief among those interventions are the plethora of federal programs. Goetze is appropriately skeptical about such programs, particularly if they are viewed as a substitute for local initiative and grassroots cooperation between neighborhood, business, and government participants.

In the late 1970s much talk was heard in Washington about federal-local "partnerships" including neighborhood folk, business, labor, and the like. But the prevailing, and possibly inevitable, mentality of "Uncle Sam knows best" proved extremely difficult to dislodge. Goetze's book may not cause reform in the bowels of the federal departments such as Housing and Urban Development, but it ought to warn city and neighborhood leaders across the country to be on guard and to assess as carefully as possible the negative as well as promised positive effects of any proffered federal program.

Rolf Goetze in no way belongs to the camp of those who would neglect the cities and their neighborhoods because of the intractability of problems there. He warmly endorses the positive model of the

Neighborhood Housing Services precisely because it is indigenous, appropriate, and partnership-based. He notes that the more frequent pattern of splintered, uncoordinated federal programs can be like dangerous drugs, leading to iatrogenic or doctor-induced illness. But rather than having the physician retreat from the field, he would have him return to the status of the family practitioner to deal with the whole patient.

To understand the whole patient, Goetze suggests some challenging ideas for obtaining better information about neighborhoods, particularly the dynamics of change within them. For example, one of these ideas uses comparable time series on computer tape in the same format for different cities. His hope is that such an information system would reveal hidden patterns and that really workable programs or approaches could be identified among the myriad of competing promises and new innovations. This book makes it clear that development of such an information system would be difficult and complex. But the effort, given the amount of often misguided urban investment now being made, seems worthwhile.

Goetze is refreshingly candid about the problem of competing values. He refuses to demagogue the displacement issue. He asks us, for instance: "Does an elderly widow have the right to retain the large rental apartment in which she raised her family when she can no longer afford it and a young couple would like it as a condominium?" It would take a Solomon to resolve that issue. Indeed, there are many issues that neither city halls, planners, nor bureaucrats at any level should claim to have answers for. Illustrating the complexity of neighborhood revival, Goetze on one hand cautions us about the "Super-Haves"—pace-setters, not now producing children, and therefore not interested in safe yards and good schools, but rather in urban amenities, chic dress, good food, exotic travel and me, me, me. Yet in recounting the story of Boston's Ashmont Hill–Dorchester neighborhood, he tells how the decision of 150 or so affluent persons to buy and restore has led countless other residents from nearby sections of Dorchester to say to themselves, "If those with college degrees are buying that close to Roxbury, then we've got many years to look forward to here." As a result, they shift their "scheming time" away from a new place to move toward home improvements, savings, and the like. New resources of community pride emerge, revitalizing a substantial part of a city.

All too much of the national debate about cities and neighborhoods has centered on their sicknesses. This book is an opening wedge into looking at the dynamics of change, to see how positive impulses can be harnessed and negative ones sidetracked. Correctly, the focus is on the psychology of neighborhood life—whether residents believe (and are told by the media) that their area is hopeless, on the decline, a place to escape from, or quite the reverse; a place on the upswing, where they feel free to make fresh investments, to start the neighborhood clean-ups and community activities that make a neighborhood a strong and healthy place to live.

In his earlier works, Goetze dealt with the phenomenon of the post World War II baby boom and its impact on the housing market. In *Stabilizing Neighborhoods*, he treated us to the metaphor of tsunami accounts—"how a tidal wave first pulls the waters way back exposing the hidden ocean floor, before rushing in swamping everything in sight." He told us that in recent years we have been "puzzled, exploring the mysterious ocean floor and arguing about questions of neighborhood blight, lack of mortgage credit, and dwindling city revenues. When the tidal wave of new households engulfs urban areas," he wrote, "most of the existing housing supply will be brought into play because the nation simply cannot produce enough housing in the next fifteen or twenty years to meet the new demand."

In this book, Goetze returns to the baby boom phenomenon. He ties it to the dynamics of the housing industry and the pattern that began around 1960 of overproduction of housing that actually caused urban distress by luring young people into starter homes in new subdivisions instead of looking for opportunities in older neighborhoods. His charts show that in the coming years, the tidal wave will result in a tight market that will rapidly end "the era of planned obsolescence, the 'throw-away society'." And then, in a delightful figure of speech, he likens the baby boom to the bulge of a watermelon swallowed by a boa constrictor, moving slowly through the reptile from 1950s' preoccupation with child-rearing and schools to a predicted 1980s' focus on home ownership, the cost of housing, and increasing conservatism as people question whether government provides them an appropriate return on their tax dollars. Writing in the late 1970s, one is tempted to say that Goetze's vision of the 1980s is already upon us. But it will not, Goetze suggests, promise us automatic prosperity in our city neighborhoods unless there is appropriate public policy to avoid the extremes of displacement or decline.

What will such public policy have to be? Goetze's "Housing Policy Law" is deceptively simple: to maintain predictable relationships between housing benefits and costs for all interests; to be fair and predictable to all actors in the system; to avoid unnecessary and disturbing complexity, especially through a succession of "innovative" but often contradictory government interventions.

Does that sound like overly meek counsel? I think not. Viewing the baby boom, the renewed push for city locations, and the dangers of overheated housing markets, Goetze suggests that such traditional urban planning tools as mortgage, construction subsidies, and rental assistance are "like pebbles in these new demographic tides." Refreshingly, Goetze is one of the few urban commentators today who would try to aid cities to turn the new developments to their advantage rather than to depend heavily on federal assistance. He believes sensible planning and coordinated efforts can put "a tailwind" behind the forces of neighborhood revitalization. That approach sounds modest, and it may be. It may also be the only rational course for the 1980s.

Neal R. Peirce
Syndicated Urban Affairs
Columnist and Contributing Editor
National Journal

Acknowledgments

If you stand in one spot long enough and note what is going on around you, imperceptible changes become evident that escape the attention of others hurrying about their business. This kind of observation can be rewarding. People talk to you. Others seek you out because you were there at some point in the past that has suddenly become important to them. If you help them retrieve what they failed to note at the time, they immediately consider you an expert and send others to you.

As you add these pieces to your own observations, insights emerge and a transformation sets in. A birdwatcher presumably becomes an ecologist when he notices that the usual bird population is disappearing and questions why. Only then can he discover that their eggshells have become too thin for reproduction, and that the DDT being passed up the food chain is responsible for the impending "silent spring."

Neighborhood watching affords similar opportunities and experiences, but there is a special twist: the most interesting data are those that conventional research discards as unsuitable for further processing. An absurd sales price here, a tangled title there, a lone architecture student seeking a slum to fix up—such bits provide significant clues to neighborhood change.

This book continues where *Building Neighborhood Confidence* left off in developing a fresh approach to understanding housing dynamics and neighborhood revitalization.

The insights come from so many people that it is difficult to thank them all. The book springs from a continuing commitment to professional urban research that has been led by Alex Ganz, director of research at the Boston Redevelopment Authority under three directors: Robert T. Kenney, Robert F. Walsh, and most recently, Robert J. Ryan. Without their support, perceptive neighborhood watching could never have developed. Among the many colleagues in this endeavor, Bonnie Heudorfer, Lowell Richards, John Avault, Andrew Olins, Craig Nickerson, Jim Carras, and Tim Pattison deserve special mention. Many of the inspirations can be traced to interactions with the *Living in Boston* team that promotes Boston's neighborhoods, Bob Rugo and John Coggeshall, led by John Weis.

Tunney Lee, Rob Hollister, Phil Clay, Kent Colton, and their students have reacted to and improved many of the rough ideas in discussions at the MIT Neighborhood Colloquia.

Watchers in other cities have also helped focus these observations. These include Robert Kuttner of the National Commission on Neighborhoods, Marilyn Burckhardt of New York, Barbara Chance of Philadelphia, Richard Taub and Ron Gryzwinski of Chicago, Sam White of Milwaukee, Alan Canter of Denver, Tom Vitek and George Williams of San Francisco, David Lewis of Los Angeles, Don de la Peña of San Jose, Jim King of Palo Alto, Rona Zevin and William Stafford of Seattle, Jill Diskan of Hartford, and Richard Hanel with the R.L. Polk Company in Detroit.

Vince O'Donnell and Catherine Carroll each helped in our many housing research efforts. Robert Fichter of Boston's Parkman Center and Patrick Hare of Hartford were especially helpful, sparking fresh insights as individual chapters began to take shape. As these, in turn, grew into a longer and more turgid manuscript, Tom Chmura, Steve Waldhorn, and John Sawyer helped pick out the basic threads when I lost them.

Throughout this long and often tedious process my wife Julie Anne helped edit and revise, patiently typed and retyped sections, suggested improvements, and cheerfully encouraged me to complete the book, even as it continued to consume more and more of our evenings and weekends.

I accept the blame for any errors, omissions, or oversimplifications I may have made in my eagerness to introduce readers to these new concepts. Since the sources of inspiration cannot always be traced, I also apologize in advance to any and all I may have inadvertently left out.

Rolf Goetze
Belmont, Massachusetts

**Understanding
Neighborhood
Change**

 *Chapter 1*

Introduction

Changes in the workings of the housing market are remaking the face of America's neighborhoods. Because these changes have hardly been explored, planners, policymakers, and the public are confused as to how urban areas might best be revitalized. While housing demand now surges in many parts of the country, abandonment often continues in these very areas. In some urban areas newly built public housing is deteriorating or requires continually greater subsidies to avoid foreclosure. At the same time neglected properties only a few blocks away are already reviving without public assistance and in spite of bank red-lining, conferring windfall gains upon their discoverers. For the first time in recent memory there is serious competition for some of the urban living space already occupied by those less well off.

While federal policy has tended to view housing as an income problem, others have discovered that credit availability and neighborhood confidence exert critical influences on housing improvement and deterioration. These issues present challenging enigmas. A comprehensive theory is required to replace the current piecemeal efforts using outmoded programs and policy tools to prevent gentrification and displacement in one area while subsidizing rehabilitation nearby.

A fresh conceptual framework to recast neighborhood change and new kinds of data are also needed before productive housing policies can be agreed upon. The purpose of this book is to develop and explore these new concepts of neighborhood change—its determinants, corollaries, and consequences.

PLANNING IS COPING WITH CHANGE

People are impatient to know what will work. However, it is more important first to recognize what no longer works and why. The idea that household income and filtration govern neighborhood change is still generally accepted, but this no longer suffices to explain increasingly sharp dynamics. Until the 1960s, housing market fluctuations could be overlooked as minor when compared to filtration. But since then the trickling down of older housing to lower income residents has become irregular and unpredictable, particularly in large cities. No longer do all neighborhoods seem to follow steady, straight-line trends as they mature. Already the limited data available suggest that neighborhood futures are no longer predictable on the basis of appraisers' estimates of remaining economic life or available resident incomes.

The basic planning issue is coping with change, but what is desirable or undesirable change is no longer easily defined. While neighborhood change is taking on new dimensions with the resurgence of interest in urban living, local leaders and decisionmakers are unconsciously adhering to outmoded assumptions and inappropriate ethics.

As complexity increases, politicians and bureaucrats shift too easily from managing change to masking it, attempting to preserve the status quo, or demonstrating that something can be done, even as the altered system makes it less and less possible. Better data and more comprehensive theory are required if urban policy is to break out of this complexity trap. Better neighborhood data and analysis will assist in the earlier detection of actual neighborhood trends, the development of a more appropriate theory of neighborhood evolution, and the discovery of more constructive public interventions.

INFORMATION BLOCKAGES
AND INCREASED COMPLEXITY

Changes on the urban scene are increasingly obscured by complexity and compounded by new information blockages. Information that traditionally flowed between participants no longer does so as readily, thus creating new housing market imperfections. The costs of acquiring information have increased sharply, and greater effort is required to assure its transmission. As mistrust grows, many interest groups question the reliability and currency of information. At the same time, information has become a scarce resource that confers power to those who possess it. Hence issues over control of data erupt along with debates over everyone's rights to privacy. Finally, even when information is available, the ability and willingness to use it are often missing.

In urban areas the simplistic response to increasing complexity has been to call for greater participation, neighborhood capacity building, government intervention, and financial assistance. As the number of participants grows, each strives for greater control, not realizing what the tug of war is about. Neighborhood organization has become romanticized, but it more often represents desperation—an heroic response to the complexity and insensitivity of bureaucracy.

A primary result of increased complexity is that everyone loses sight of the big picture. Uncertainty grows as people can no longer tell in what direction things are going. This discourages investors and entrepreneurs. It also leads to red-lining and the desire by bankers and insurors to have the government back them to guarantee risks.

Complexity also blurs accountability for the actions of different participants in the system. When our forebears built their shelters and heat was inadequate, each had only himself or fate to blame. They chopped more wood and prayed. Even as people urbanized, rights and responsibilities remained clearly defined between tenants and landlords. However, as the public sector entered into housing provision and production, responsibilities have become diffused and accountability lost.

Complexity has therefore made exploitation easier. Only the more sophisticated and unscrupulous know how to achieve their self-interest by finding loopholes and outwitting bureaucrats. The blurring of accountability has not succeeded in correcting market imperfections.

PERCEPTIONS, EXPECTATIONS, AND THE MEDIA

Red-lining, disinvestment, gentrification, displacement, reinvestment, incumbent upgrading, value inflation, speculation, flipping, and most ambiguous of all, revitalization are all new media buzzwords used to describe the changes. As yet, few of these terms have rigorous or commonly accepted definitions. Instead, they signal the emergence of new issues and questions of fairness as each hearer defines them his own way. Is red-lining withholding people's money from their own neighborhoods so that banks can earn profits in new subdivisions elsewhere, or is it simply the wise exercise of fiduciary responsibility not to throw good money after bad? When is displacement simply normal dwelling turnover, and when is the takeover of a dwelling by another who can afford to pay more unfair? The interrelationships of these new terms must be explored, for without sharply defined terminology and better measures of change, such issues only lend themselves to endless debate—grist for politicians and news stories perhaps, but not for equitable resolution.

Expectations have become untethered from reality. When members of the American family reach for their portion of the proverbial pie, it is still assumed each sees his share in relation to the whole and to others' portions and is either content with the share or tries to work out the inequities. However, many more individuals now simply receive slices from the kitchen. Few are aware of how much is actually available, but they clearly see some slices as much larger than others. They then attempt to get a better share or to control distribution. Such preoccupations lead to bitterness, mistrust, and dissatisfaction among individuals when in fact each could live well on his portion.

As everyone's share falls short of expectations, citizens invite the government even further into their lives to determine and insure property values, produce housing, provide credit, and support bankrupt developments or possibly even bankrupt cities. Outmoded assumptions, media distortions, and reflections of the past now guide policymaking. Complexity and information blockages discourage wider understanding of the current system while urban research is thwarted by the unavailability of hard data. The media interpret events, influence behavior, and indirectly set priorities in this context of rapid change and uncertainty, complexity, and lack of information.

What is a house in the city now worth? What determines its value? When the banks will not lend conventionally because their appraisers are nervous, are the properties less valuable? Do they become more valuable when the government insures the mortgages completely or devises a new type of mortgage? Is a mortgage a right?

A mortgage was once a simple agreement between lender and borrower spelling out the terms and responsibilities of each. A borrower rented the use of capital as lenders judged the risks themselves. Now bankers often provide credit in marginal neighborhoods only when the government guarantees the loans. Red-lining signalled that traditional yardsticks had become useless and that lenders were unsure how things would turn out. Instead of developing new yardsticks, people turned to the government.

Urban neighborhood futures can be seen as halfway gone or halfway up. In large cities, particularly in the Frostbelt, residents, lenders, brokers, city officials, and potential buyers generally saw many urban neighborhoods as already half gone. The media focus on abandoned houses, crime, and poverty fostered these beliefs, perhaps unwittingly. Only a few independents among the young and better educated saw things differently. Currently the awareness of new urban promise diffuses only slowly and uncertainly in most older cities. Here complexity makes it difficult to persuade most of the residents in time for them to share in the benefits of revitalization by taking title to their homes. Often they only believe it after the local media have heralded the resurgence of confidence, and when it is already evident in house tours, startling appreciation, or historic district designation. Then suddenly too many seek entry, overheating the local market and making displacement likely.

It seems that as the local bureaucracies become more tangled and confused, neighborhood confidence increasingly ebbs and flows. First red tape and uncertainty blight neighborhoods. Then strong, pent-up housing demand, whose existence was unrecognized, surges into enclaves discovered by independents, producing spot gentrification. Clarity of local policy determines whether gentrifying hot spots result or a more generally beneficial uplift of neighborhood confidence occurs.

The ethic of "rights based on needs" clashes with a more basic American ethic, "I earned it, I deserve it." The political clamor for redress here challenges the reward ethic. Interest groups now stake out ideological positions, frequently unaware of changed or changing realities. To focus the debate, the new urban terrain must be charted and reference points for monitoring change must be developed so that everyone—from neighborhood activist to official policymaker— can determine, in a timely way, where particular neighborhoods are positioned and headed. In too many cities government policymakers have not done this; instead they have masked the changes.

RECENT GOVERNMENT PROGRAMS

Past public efforts have attempted to address the symptoms directly. If the private sector does not provide enough housing, the government promises to build and provide it for only one quarter of household income—a promise too good to deliver to all. If the banks will not lend for home improvements, the government will provide low interest loans. This raises expectations but exacerbates matters when, as it always turns out, there is not enough to go around. How does the home improver, about to borrow at 12 percent interest, feel when he hears of others getting low interest government money? He often stops and decides to wait to get his share. If he thinks the distribution is unfair or that the recipients are less deserving, then he, too, joins the debate.

In too many cities, simple political promises raise expectations. Complexity, together with persuasiveness of the media, prevents the public from seeing that these expectations can never be equitably met. To an outsider it is already evident that America's urban needs have become redefined so generously that available means are quite inadequate to meet expectations. However, most insiders remain either unaware of the futility of their best efforts or do not know how to improve matters.

Innovative programs are started because politicians attain office through promise and hold it by showing effort, not through results. The urgent need to do something in spite of inadequate means has created a strange symbiosis among politicians, bureaucrats, and the media. Artificial demonstrations are heralded as innovative break-throughs, but in fact they can never be reproduced spontaneously. Many unilateral government programs that promise to act as pump primers instead increase dependency on public assistance. Currently no mechanisms such as sunset laws exist to eliminate programs or agencies that once were the promising efforts of previous administrations but now only complicate matters in order to survive.

Cynics argue that government has now compounded Parkinson's Laws with the Peter Principle and Gresham's Law: As the government work force expands to consume the resources available, the individuals are promoted to their level of incompetence, and the bad drive out the good. Optimists thereupon point out that California's Proposition 13 has injected a healthy skepticism into continued public spending just as a flood of young households independently revitalizes some city areas that local officials had consigned to blight. In any case, a confusing tangle of conflicting and unequal interests has developed, each pressing forward without adequate feedback on its beneficial or harmful impact upon the others. This situation has been some time in the making.

Hindsight suggests that private overproduction of housing in the 1960s spurred urban abandonment and that assisting production was a mistake. Yet the theory of filtration was then so widely held that LBJ's Great Society and the Kaiser Commission believed increasing government production was the way to eliminate substandard housing.

More recently ecological awareness, energy concerns, anti-growth, citizen participation, minority hiring, and conservation movements have entered the picture. No one really knows how these movements now constrain housing production through laws, prices, bureaucracies, and people's preferences. However, production has become constrained as record numbers of new households seek to settle down, promising to raise sharply the value of everything already built.

Some now argue that no government programs could have had much impact in the face of these dynamics. Others point out that their impact has been substantial but counterintuitive, that is, the inadvertent spillovers of public programs on bystanders have often turned out to be far more significant and negative than the promised benefits heralded by the media that led to their creation. In any case, government programs have generally been accepted under the presumption that they will at least improve, if not correct, situations. While no data are available to prove or disprove the efficacy of government programs, more people are beginning to suspect that they mask failures. Many government programs are no longer solutions but have become a major part of the problem. As policymakers pursue amelioration of symptoms, underlying causes are increasingly obscured and thereby gain more momentum. It is late and difficult to see where policy can go from here.

NEW DIRECTIONS FOR POLICYMAKERS

Housing supply and demand imbalances must be analyzed, understood, and corrected. Public expectations must be tempered with reality, and interventions must be recast to work indirectly at the margins. Each of these fundamental new directions merits elaboration here.

In some regions, when housing demand exceeds the available supply, a competitive struggle develops for the available quarters causing deep stresses to the entire urban region. The symptoms of these new stresses are not easily recognized as fundamentally different from the deterioration linked to overproduction. However, here the generation-old but unfulfilled promise of a decent, affordable home in a suitable living environment will become unattainable for an increasing number, not only for minorities and the poor. Traditional child-raising families with only one wage earner will feel disadvantaged as two incomes become necessary for attaining home ownership. Alienation, mistrust, and conflict are likely to increase among different interests on this score. As the urban neighborhoods are rediscovered, critical new tests of fairness will erupt. Does an elderly widow have the right to retain the large rental apartment in which she raised her family when she can no longer afford it and a young couple would like it as a condominium?

In other regions, when there is a housing surplus in the face of slack demand, strategies for planned shrinkage must be developed despite the political unattractiveness of such an undertaking. This will be necessary even if a few neighborhoods gentrify.

Everywhere, the changing balance between supply and demand must be monitored at the regional, city, and local levels, and imbalances prevented whenever possible so that speculation or disinvestment do not undermine neighborhood confidence.

Redistributing excess housing demand—guiding and diffusing gentrification in areas where there is overall balance—emerges as a constructive new role for policymakers. Improvements in general welfare become more likely by steering buyers away from the fashionable neighborhoods toward weaker ones than by intervening directly with the housing assistance tools of the 1960s.

The partnership among the politicians, the bureaucrats, and the media must be stopped from touting elaborately contrived housing demonstrations as breakthroughs when they cannot actually be easily replicated.

Resident expectations must then be openly addressed. Planners must first determine the kind and amount of resources actually available. If too many expect more than their share, this will raise difficulties, which become quite serious if some succeed in obtaining what others see as an inordinate share. Because it is now so much easier to oppose actions that seem unfair than to initiate programs, efforts without deep public support will become increasingly costly and difficult. This has contributed to the soaring costs of assisted housing production.

The most effective housing actions work indirectly through influencing and facilitating the countless but necessary interactions among provider, consumer, lender, investor, buyer, and seller. These actions are neither glamorous nor direct and they are time consuming. In the media-dominated, result-oriented society this presents a problem, but the rhetoric that is mistaken for policy formulation is frequently counterproductive. Reform and deregulation are much more important than erecting new programs. Currently the system provides few incentives for pursuing this course, but if followed it would allow many situations to mend themselves. Concern for the disadvantaged should be translated into providing them with the know-how and resources directly rather than through subsidized providers and caretakers.

Mortgage review boards, some Neighborhood Housing Services initiatives, and other Urban Revitalization Task Force concepts work successfully because they temper expectations with reality. By reexamining the traditional roles and responsibilities of every interest, results are often achieved that conventional thinkers did not deem possible. Many more such instances where the public sector effectively complements local aspirations, joining public, private, and community interests, are waiting to be discovered. The most likely initiatives to succeed in the near future will be those that have taken into account how each affected interest will interpret its benefits and drawbacks.

The 1980s offer a rare opportunity for developing a new urbanism. Demographic trends are very favorable to rejuvenate urban neighborhoods. Many marginal neighborhoods can now go up as easily as down. In the current complexity, expectations are likely to be self-fulfilling. In instances where residents expect deterioration to continue and public interventions to be futile, they will turn out that way. On the other hand when people expect a marginal neighborhood to improve, they behave accordingly, and it improves.

In the longer run a new policy approach is needed. This book makes the case for a basic new housing policy law: The long-term housing benefits and costs attached to any public intervention must remain predictable and seem fair to every interest. This raises two fundamental challenges to current planning practice: (1) replacing outworn assumptions about what works, and (2) fine-tuning policymakers' awareness to respond to the new neighborhood realities. If these challenges can be overcome, a remarkable number of urban neighborhoods will revitalize virtually on their own.

The following chapters address the themes identified above. The book is divided into three parts. The first part, Chapters 2 and 3, concentrates on monitoring and analyzing neighborhood change. The second part, Chapters 4, 5, and 6, outlines a new theory of neighborhood dynamics, stressing the new economic and social forces currently at work in neighborhoods. The last part, Chapters 7, 8, and 9, explores the self-protective symbiosis that has developed among bureaucrats, politicians, and the media, recognizing that this is where citizens must change the system if general welfare is to improve.

Chapter 2

Changing Neighborhoods: Different Perceptions and Shifting Trends

This chapter provides an overview. It examines how neighborhood perceptions vary and also how they change with time. It explores the shifting national demographic context behind these issues and concludes with five major inferences.

SHIFTING NEIGHBORHOOD PERCEPTIONS

Imagine that the Smiths want to buy an urban property in which to live. They begin with newspaper broker listings and spot a good lead:

> Three-family, good condition
> 220 wiring, excel. investment
> opportunity—low 20s

The broker wastes little time on them, just telling them where the house is located. When they go out to look at the property they encounter Mrs. Murphy, who has lived next door for years. "Did you hear of last week's hold-up at the drug store?" she asks. "Isn't it awful, what's happening?" She has been in the neighborhood for years and implies that she deserves better than what the neighborhood has come to.

Undaunted, the Smiths go to a bank where they are told that only government-insured mortgages with points are available even though they have the down payment for the home and intend to live there. They phone the broker again to find out who is buying in the neighborhood. "Mostly blue collar outsiders, buying as an investment," he tells them, "plus a stray gay or two, and, oh yes, an interracial couple, and, ah, one of those communes."

The Smiths lose interest in this neighborhood. They go back to the newspaper listings where they find another prospect:

> Handyman's dream, three-family
> with original oak woodwork;
> unlimited possibilities for
> the creative buyer—mid 20s

The broker takes them out to the property and tells them that a young diamond merchant and a state planner have bought homes nearby. And the neighborhood homes tour last month was covered in the Sunday paper. Mrs. White, a nosey, long-term resident, had been listening and interrupts. "But I don't understand why those new young couples would buy here," she says. "They seem nice enough, but I wish they'd have children. That binds a marriage."

While the Smiths are still mulling over the possibility of making an offer, a snappier listing catches their eye:

> A real gem, Victorian triple-decker
> with unique stained glass
> stair lights, orig. gas fixtures
> intact—low 30s

By the time they phone the broker, this one is already sold. That makes them eager to see one like it. While it costs a good deal more, they feel it would be wise to buy in a neighborhood with strong housing demand.

HOW URBAN NEIGHBORHOOD PERCEPTIONS CHANGE

When we realize the foregoing is a description of the same neighborhood in 1970, 1974, and 1978, we can draw some conclusions:

- Desirability is contagious. The Smiths felt that since no one like them was buying in the neighborhood in 1970, it was undesirable, while the quick sale of the "Victorian gem" in 1978 made them eager.

- Different brokers match up with different client types. The broker showing the neighborhood in 1970 knew either that the Smiths were unlikely to buy or that they were not his kind. By 1978 a different broker was on the scene.

- Most residents accept the dominant view of the neighborhood as broadcast by the media. But if the message is negative they attempt to set themselves apart. Mrs. Murphy told the Smiths about the hold-up and wanted them to feel sorry for her, but they would never have known of the hold-up had she not told them.

- The lenders were unsure about urban neighborhoods in 1970. But the red-lining issue and mortgage disclosure brought reconsideration. However, just as bankers were blamed for red-lining, they may now be blamed for "displacement" since they make mortgages available to the young, affluent homebuyer.

- New buyers should be watched because they will set the tone and comprise the future body of residents. The neighborhood, then, changed hands—from pioneers, gays, and interracial couples, to the early adopters (diamond merchant and state planner) to a flood of twenty-six to thirty-nine-year-old joiners (newly formed middle class households eager to give city living a try).

- The media, both television and newspapers, have increasingly shaped perceptions about the neighborhood. It was first seen as a place where drugstores were held up, then where crowds attended a house tour, and finally where trend-setters created a new urban life style in renovated Victorian structures.

These stories have come to stand for the neighborhood in each individual's mind since he has fewer and fewer first-hand dealings there.

The degree to which these items shape our perception of the neighborhood is seldom recognized. Table 2–1 shows these changes in perception from various viewpoints.

CONSEQUENCES OF THE CHANGING NATIONAL DEMOGRAPHIC CONTEXT

Some explanation for these changes in urban neighborhoods as well as some hints of coming trends can be found by comparing changes in the rate of growth of both national housing demand and supply. Serious mismatches show up. During the 1960s housing production soared while the fewer children born during the Depression reached the age of settling down. This period is characterized by overproduction and urban blight. In the 1980s, in contrast, housing promises to be in very short supply.

The rate of growth in demand between 1900 and 1950 was steady compared to recent fluctuations. For those settling down in the 1960s, there was plenty of space wherever they went, in going to

Table 2–1.   Profiles of Three Neighborhoods

	Neighborhood '70	Neighborhood '74	Neighborhood '78
Real estate broker listings	• 3 Family in good condition, 220 wiring, excl. investment opportunity—low 20s	• Handyman's dream: 3 Family with original oak woodwork; unlimited possibilities for the creative buyer—mid 20s	• A Real Gem: Victorian Triple-Decker with unique stained glass stair lights, orig. gas fixtures intact—low 30s
Long-term resident views	"The schools, crime, and taxes are certainly getting to me. If I could afford to leave I would."	"I can't see why those new, young couples would buy here. They seem nice enough, though I wish they'd have children—that binds a marriage."	I like the way the Joneses have fixed up the old corner house. Why don't we redo our kitchen and heating? We could borrow against our life insurance." OR "I'm worried they are going to raise our taxes and we won't be able to stay here."
Lender practices	Mortgages only available from special brokers and under FHA or VA insurance, with "points" i.e. "red-lined"	Banks attempting to redefine their lending policy—e.g., conventional loans to resident-owned, single family structures only, lack of local credit for duplexes or absentee owners	Conventional credit available for buyers with good credit and down payment; government insured mortgages for those with poor credit; private mortgage insurance for those simply without down payment but having good employment prospects
New buyers	Blue collar investors and a few unconventional twenty-four to twenty-nine year old "pioneers" (with only very few young children, if any), handy, do-it-yourself, go-it alone type	Risk (and gain) conscious thirty to thirty-five year old entrepreneur couples—excited about neighborhood's possibilities, eager to set up house tours, a housing "bank" for referrals, etc.	Flood of twenty-six to thirty-nine year old "joiners"—cross-section of young, middle class households just forming and eager to give city living a try.
Media reports	"Bad news" of distressed city and urban problems like crime, failing schools, tax scandals dominate the news. Neighborhood focus features abandoned houses, park vandalism, etc. • basic tone: "Ain't it awful!"	Positive neighborhood news stories, human interest items, reviews of house tours, house bank details periodically break into "conventional" coverage; emergence of Sunday supplement stories on city living. • overtone: potential excitement	Press begins to hype new urban life styles, promoting neighborhood chic, rediscovery: "last chance to buy," "buy now or pay later." Displacement becomes new media issue (replacing red-lining) "We always knew this neighborhood would make it, but what about the displaces?" • overtone: glow and frenzy

college, looking for a job, or buying a home. For those born after 1950, it has obviously been a very different story. The numbers that will be settling down in new households in the 1980s will be enormous, almost double those of the 1960s. New trends toward childlessness may hold down reproduction as well as radically alter housing demands.

Figure 2-1 offers a simple proxy for changes in housing demand, the varying numbers of persons reaching age thirty in five-year cohorts.

Examining housing starts adds more insights. Annual building cycles show wide fluctuations, but seen in five-year totals, a pattern again emerges. The period from 1890 to 1945 averaged 400,000 housing starts a year, punctuated by reduced starts during World War I, the Depression, and World War II, and higher starts whenever prosperity permitted. In 1945, in creating the Federal Housing Administration (FHA), the nation shifted to a sustained production rate almost four times higher, an average of 1.5 million starts per year. Too many economists now view gloomily, and simplistically, any year with less than two million housing starts.

Figure 2-2 is drawn to match the population dynamics in Figure 2-1.

Overlaying the above two figures suggests that until 1945 the nation was adding less housing than households, leading to full utilization of existing opportunities. Only in the 1920s did housing starts surge. The Depression and World War II were particularly tough years of making do, so the nation was ready to turn out housing after the war. For a decade or so the stunning production unleashed in 1945 compensated for lost effort, but continuing this process into the 1960s helped bring about the era of planned obsolescence, the "throw-away society." Only in the early 1980s will demand justify two million annual housing starts.

Figure 2-3 combines the two previous graphs. The scales have been chosen to suggest their interrelationship.

It now seems that increased production may actually have increased urban distress. Since 1960 this production has been luring the young directly into starter homes in new subdivisions instead of challenging them to make their homes in existing neighborhoods.

Young households are a critical national resource. They rise to challenges; are more idealistic, inventive, and resourceful; and less demanding. And they are much less committed to a particular place to settle than older households that have put down roots. (Even habitual mover-households transplant themselves to the same type of suburban ground.) As aggregate housing demand tightened in the late

Figure 2–1. Fluctuating U.S. Housing Demand 1900–2005

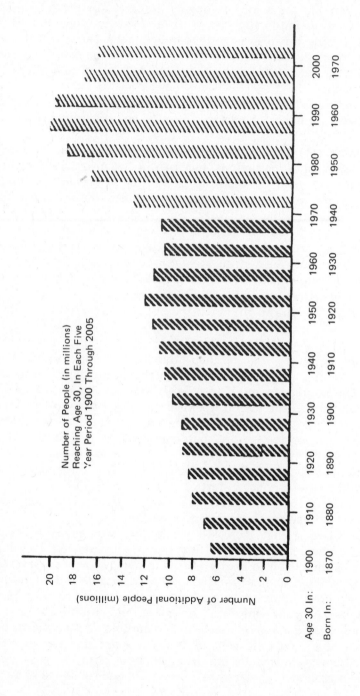

Number of People (in millions)
Reaching Age 30, In Each Five
Year Period 1900 Through 2005

Number of Additional People (millions)

Age 30 In:	1900	1910	1920	1930	1940	1950	1960	1970	1980	1990	2000
Born In:	1870	1880	1890	1900	1910	1920	1930	1940	1950	1960	1970

Source: Mass. Office of State Planning Calculations from U.S. Census.

Figure 2–2. Fluctuating U.S. Housing Starts 1890–1975

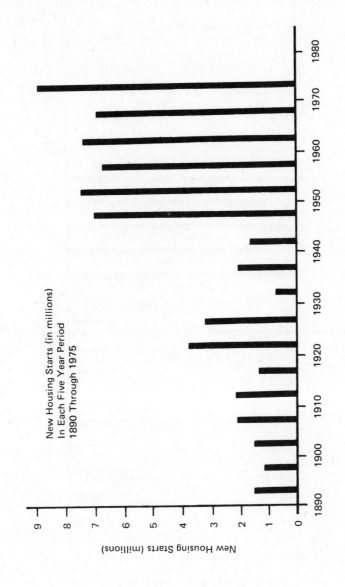

New Housing Starts (in millions)
In Each Five Year Period
1890 Through 1975

Source: Historical Statistics of the U.S. Dept. of Commerce.

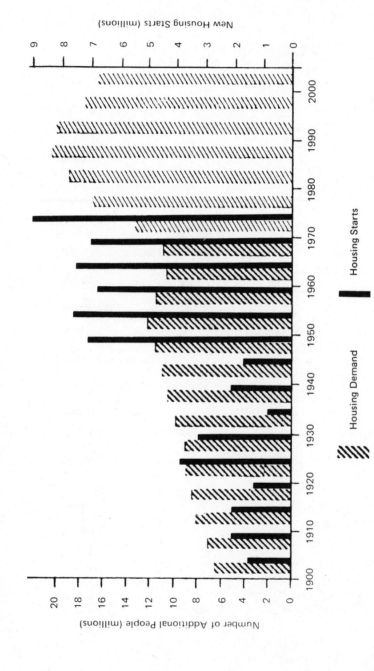

Figure 2–3. U.S. Housing Starts vs. Demand in Each Five Year Period 1900–1975

Source: Figures 2–1 and 2–2.

1970s, pioneers from the giant generation were leading the way back into urban neighborhoods.

That trend was not foreseen in 1965 when HUD was created and set out to deal with urban problems by stepping up housing production. The Kaiser Commission promised the eradication of substandard urban housing if the nation increased annual production to 2.6 million starts. The goals of the commission now suggest a grave misunderstanding of cause and effect, but this is easier to recognize in hindsight than when President Johnson, a man driven to action, sought out the Kaiser Commission goals.

Some experts now realize the disastrous nature of those past recommendations, and how lucky it was such production levels were never attained as they would have produced that much more abandonment and disinvestment. But even today many still believe that stepped-up production would eliminate substandard housing.

Shifting the housing starts graph by a generation creates Figure 2−4, which relates housing starts to the years in which people were born. This reveals a correlation between housing starts and births. Whether new homes beget children or new children drive their parents to get new homes is unclear—the circumstances nevertheless go together. The peak years in the 1920s of housing starts and child-rearing coincide. The 1945 to 1970 period also fits, especially when one considers the smaller number of children per household. But since 1970 there have been significantly more starts than babies. Does this suggest why demand is surging in many urban neighborhoods? Did trends of buying new homes continue in a kind of cultural inertia even when the new households held off on having children? Will this pattern continue? Or are children simply being postponed?

These issues are admittedly complex, confusing, and subject to debate. It seems that a national penchant has developed for simplifying complex issues via the media: one cause, one blame, one corrective program "for all that ails us." While academics take issue with the many simplifications in the above analysis, others simplify the causes of urban decline even further. The following pattern seems to be happening in many cities simultaneously (Goetze, 1977: i):

> Who caused this neighborhood to decline? Why are there broken streets, vacant houses, boarded-up stores where there was once a solid, thriving community? A middle-aged woman cannot bear the thought of a second visit to her old neighborhood—"Not after what they've done to it."

> Who are they? Well, it's obvious, isn't it? The streets are full of black faces. Black people just don't care. They've let the neighborhood go to Hell. The blacks did it.

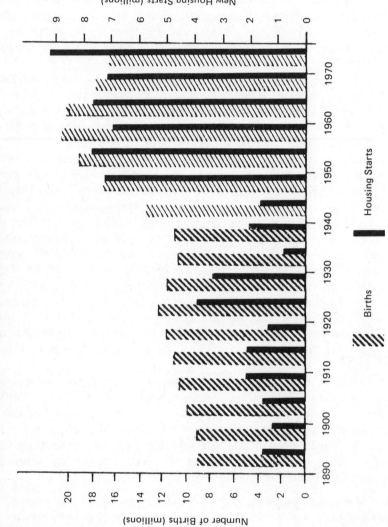

Figure 2–4. U.S. Housing Starts vs. Births in Each Five Year Period 1890–1975

Source: Figures 2–1 and 2–2.

Aha! It's explained. Look no further!

But according to a militant young staffer in a State regulatory agency, the banks did it. They've red-lined the area. By strangling the flow of mortgage money, they've made it impossible for a healthy replacement process to continue. They suck up urban deposits and deposit capital in more profitable, lower risk suburban developments. Quite clearly, the banks did it.

Aha, again! Now the culprit is found!

Not according to a bank president. If anyone deserves the blame, it is the City. The City, not the banks, is responsible for dirty streets, inequitable assessments, venal building inspectors, indifferent police.

The third "Aha" is already weaker. Is this the real culprit now?

The City now suggests the Department of Housing and Urban Development. HUD did it with its ill-conceived, mismanaged FHA low down payment home ownership program, not to mention its financially distressed 221 (d) (3) and 236 subsidized developments, or its public housing disasters.

Everyone is pointing the finger at everyone else. In this confusion various interests argue from differing premises for conflicting solutions. It's an income problem. No, it's a race problem. If the banks hadn't red-lined . . . corruption. . . .

Policymaking, in relation to these issues, has become fragmented into at least five planning roles. These are caricatured here like political cartoons to focus on the salient features. The *Community Development Block Grant Planner* sees urban problems as economic, requiring mortgage subsidies and financial finagling. He is confused about his constituency and is caught in contradictions and red tape. Yet he is a stickler for following the rules. The *ethnic advocate*, on the other hand, sees urban problems as social ones, a matter of excluding undesirable behavior, even if preserving the rights of existing residents keeps out the more disadvantaged.

The *black advocate* focuses on racism and seeks ways of changing the system to compensate for years of exploitation, neglect, and discrimination. The *historic preservationist* is the young professional excited by the aesthetic and physical challenge of restoring tarnished structures he has discovered. Finally, the *mayor* sees everything as a shifting set of political realities that test his adeptness to address the issues.

Table 2—2 suggests the role conflicts inherent in revitalizing neighborhoods.

Table 2-2.   **Five Caricatures of Neighborhood Planning Roles**

	CDBG Planner	*Ethnic Advocate*
Urban problems primarily seen as	An economic problem, requiring mortgage subsidies and financial write-downs	A social problem of controlling or excluding undesireable behavior
Deals with neighborhood as	A piece of physical geography to be "saved" under regulations promulgated in Washington	A collection of existing residents whose rights are paramount—even if preserving these rights excludes the more disadvantaged
Principal tools and tactics	• maximize subsidized assistance availability • emphasis on compliance with HUD strategies, including: HAP: Housing Assist. Plan CDBG: Comm. Dev. Bl. Grants NSA's: Neigh. Strat. Areas UDAG's: Urb. Devel. Action Grants Pockets of Poverty	• advocates increased local control of federal and state assistance programs • emphasis on confronting lenders, insurors on "redlining," etc.
Behavior	• confused about his constituency, caught in contradictions, yet stickler for rules • as the federal rules change so do the priorities of the HUD planner—e.g. targeting vs. scatteration; triage vs. aiding the neediest	• extremely sensitive to people • often takes issue with the initiatives of others and with HUD guidelines • is usually reactive in posture • urges neighborhood empowerment

MAJOR INFERENCES

Five critical inferences easily obscured in the daily give and take among competing interests in the urban arena emerge from the above analysis.

First, *the baby bulge focuses national preoccupations.* That bulge stands out like a watermelon swallowed by a constrictor, and is mov-

Table 2—2. continued

Black Advocate	Historic Preservationist	Mayor
A racial problem of overcoming years of exploitation and discrimination	An aesthetic/physical challenge of restoring tarnished structures	A shifting set of political realities testing his adeptness to appear to be on top of the issues
A piece of turf from which minority residents will be displaced by a rising tide of urban property values	An irreplaceable collection of historically valuable structures to be restored in keeping with their original style as far as possible	A set of people with votes to be won
• attempts to define a societal/political obligation to aid blacks to compensate for past years of exploitation/ neglect	• seeking funds and the individuals necessary "to do it right," as well as historic designation for prime sites and structures	• influence, special projects patronage, ribbon-cutting • controls public budget and capital improvements
• seeking ways of retaining black rights to a rising (gentrifying) neighborhood	• can pursue quite unconventional initiatives, e.g. selling shares in neighborhoods to raise capital, taking options on prime structures before they rise in value, etc.	
• appears to be acting outside the system and often by-passed by other minority advocates • ambivalent about working within the system • seeks ways of reinterpreting the rights of minorities	• develops "clout" • gets things done • often overrides the concerns of others (espec. minority and/ or lower class needs)	• seeks to lead the maximum number of followers • • will enthusiastically embrace any idea whose time has clearly come (but not before) • pragmatic about issues

ing along, growing older. In the 1950s, the baby bulge focused our preoccupations on child raising; in the 1960s on Haight-Ashbury, Vietnam, and Woodstock; and in the 1970s on employment and the ERA. For the 1980s the focus will shift toward home ownership, the cost of housing, increasing conservatism, questioning taxes and the return on government spending. By the 1990s the bulge will be in its forties and individuals will probably be questioning the meaning of life. And finally, well after the year 2000, the question might be, who will pay old age pensions?

Second, *conflict among urban interests promises to increase.* The traditional suburban household is already no longer dominant. Many still picture an expanding suburban horizon with new homemakers settling down, producing 2.7 children, and leaving problems behind. In such a family with an income of over $20,000, the per capita income is only $5,000; but it is becoming a minority. Among the many new types of households, the Super-Haves stand out, with every member earning better than $15,000. These are pace-setters, not now bearing children, and therefore not interested in safe yards and good schools but rather in urban amenities, chic dress, good food, exotic travel, and me, me, me.

At the same time, ecological concerns of recent years have produced strong growth controls that drive up the cost of new housing production. Now some Super-Haves as well as some Haves are interested in urban neighborhoods currently occupied by Have-Nots. A sharp clash between these residents and newcomers is shaping up. All with dependents will be at a disadvantage, but especially the poor. The existing residents stress their rights and prior claim on the basis of need for the scarce resources promised by the federal government. The newcomers are embracing the ethic "I earned it, therefore I deserve it now."

This conflict is captured by a recent Boston *Real Paper* article titled "Buy Now, or Pay Later." It described an eight-room house, that Victorian gem, with one room safely storing the ten-speed racers, another for the darkroom, and still another for stereo-produced chamber music, but none for kids. The traditional family can no longer even afford to rent it. The new homeowners were the youth who were involved in civil rights, who marched at Selma, but now pursue the earn/deserve ethic while the disadvantaged, HUD, and liberals are left to ponder needs and rights in light of past failures and dwindling resources. It seems the ever-expanding pie of opportunities has slowed, leading to fights about the size of the slices.

Third, *there are inherent opportunities in this for urban areas.* Net taxpayers, who pay more in taxes than they cost to service, are re-entering cities. In 1970 the media message about cities was "only Have-Nots and unlucky people live in urban neighborhoods." Now, as there is an unexpected shift in the conventionally expected pattern of suburbanization and downward housing filtration, the suburbs suddenly appear tarnished. Urban neighborhoods are the new frontier and urban actors will be on center stage.

Fourth, *public policy roles will be reexamined.* Under current trends, disinvestment threatens to worsen in some urban neighborhoods as speculation breaks out in others. Public policy can be constructive and more effective if it focuses on the following objectives:

- Simplify and clarify the "rules of the game." The era of ever new public programs and proliferating regulations that discourage private initiative may be over as their longer term urban impact— increased confusion and uncertainty—emerges;

- Spread the new housing demand around to weaker neighborhoods to prevent golden ghettos of Super-Haves and speculation in anticipation of their coming;

- Foster more private housing maintenance and appropriate private housing production in cities as well as suburbs. This must be achieved *indirectly* through market mechanisms, not through programs that override or contradict market signals;

- Find ways to encourage neighborhood confidence and positive feelings in weaker urban neighborhoods so homeowners no longer feel further investment is unwise;

- Enable existing residents to remain if they wish, in ways that are equitable, but will not break the federal treasury;

- Develop fair measures to tax windfalls in housing appreciation and to reward longer term resident ownership. At the same time develop better investments for risk capital than speculating in scarce existing housing stock.

All this public policy effort is necessary because the new market dynamics contain a paradox: the scarcer the sought-after neighborhoods, the more desirable they appear and the more people they attract, overheating the market and conferring windfall gains to those brokering the change. For some reason, demand does not naturally diffuse to the surroundings.

The final point concerns displacement, one of the symptoms of the conflict mentioned above. The debate has already been joined without common definitions. Most become concerned and call it displacement when families are forced to move by sharply increased tax bills or hiked rents. However, a few are already concerned and call it displacement any time a household of two replaces a household of four, or a household with better income prospects replaces a poorer household. This is difficult to distinguish from the constant ups and downs of housing markets. Most of the debate about displacement engages speakers at different points on the continuum between these two definitions. There is yet a third meaning of displacement: it may be a distress call used by activists to bring policymakers to attention. Here it means simply, "help."

If one focuses too narrowly on displacement, house by house, beneficial spillovers are overlooked. In Boston, on Ashmont Hill, a newly christened part of Dorchester, perhaps 150 new households have discovered exceptional housing (obviously displacing those who might otherwise have been there). But throughout many other sections of Dorchester—Neponset, Lower Mills, Cedar Grove, and Codman Hill—there are thousands of homeowners and tenants who take their cue from the 150 saying to themselves, "If those with college degrees are buying that close to Roxbury, then we've got many years to look forward to here."

This slows the turnover and exodus. Instead of contemplating where to move, many residents now use their scheming time to consider home improvements and how to borrow against their savings, pensions, or life insurance policies. Hence a small, unexpected inmigration has brought about a very sharp change in how these people view their own neighborhoods—and it has tapped unrecognized hidden resources to help revitalize these neighborhoods.

Chapter 3

Neighborhood Monitoring
and Analysis

To improve upon the vague, ambiguous sentiment that things should be different requires developing a terminology, defining parameters for measuring change, and analyzing the actual trends taking place. Only this way can we reach agreement as to which changes are in the public interest and which interventions are appropriate.

SOME OFTEN OVERLOOKED ASPECTS
OF DATA COLLECTING

There is general consensus that planning cannot proceed in 1979 with 1970 census data. At best, the data can only provide a base to be modified by information on recent stock and household changes. But there is little agreement on how to proceed to bridge the data gap. Many cities have individually attempted to build and maintain current information systems on their housing stock and populations by integrating information from various sources: building permits, property values and assessments, vacancies, tax status, employment and unemployment, mortgage data, loan availability, housing conditions, violations and abatements, type of structure and tenure, as well as others. What initially looks promising too often becomes a bewildering swamp of data.

Several important shortcomings underlie most of these data collection efforts:

1. Data collecting can become an end in itself. Guided by a naive belief that more data are always better, collection and electronic manipulations become preoccupations as the original purposes for collecting the data slip from view. Properly, data collection makes sense only when guided by an accepted theory or when searching for fresh hypotheses in new patterns in the data.

2. Data collection becomes an escape from political heat. Wherever scarce resources are involved and policy is unclear, political debate is likely. Because economic efficiency is incompatible with equity, controversy surrounds efforts to aid the disadvantaged. Building sophisticated information systems can become a refuge rather than a policy tool.

3. It is often unclear whether data are being collected for descriptive or prescriptive purposes. For example, disclosed data on mortgage patterns by geographic area are often interpreted with the intent of pursuing retribution through future credit allocation. Prescriptions that come before understanding are usually misguided yet few probe into more subtle differences that correlate with outstanding loan balances such as differential rates of market turnover or differing cultural tendencies to pay off the mortgage. At this stage, where understanding is so limited, *describing* is more appropriate than *prescribing*.

4. Competition in data collection leads to continual improvements, that is, modifications that destroy the possibilities of developing any reliable time series. For example, there is often ambiguity in vacancy rates—when is a structure vacant and when is it abandoned? Inevitable inconsistencies among competing surveys obscure any actual trends in vacancy rates.

When HUD, in 1975, began to advocate the widespread use of R.L. Polk data to update 1970 census statistics, the effort failed for many of the above reasons. The Polk data were difficult to reconcile with local efforts already underway for tracking modifications to the 1970 census base. In general, it was simpler to disregard Polk, and in cities where Polk indicated an unexpectedly low total population, fear of cutbacks in federal aid on this account constituted "double jeopardy."

Indiscriminate data collection and the building of local data systems have not led to any universal information system or to any common language enabling various cities to compare experiences. Clearly, useful data collection must be guided by some principles.

THE INADEQUACIES OF SINGLE CONTINUUM MODELS OF NEIGHBORHOOD CHANGE

The belief that neighborhoods can be placed on a single linear continuum has long been in currency. The best known study, *Dynamics of Neighborhood Change* (HUD, 1975), ranked neighborhoods from Stage 1, stable and viable, to Stage 5, unhealthy and nonviable. This was on the right track because it put a national focus on neighborhood context, but it was too simple to be directly useful. Neighborhood rediscovery was asserted to be simply reverse filtration in this model, but closer inspection has revealed that various types of revitalization have entirely different dynamics. The many points of difference are raised throughout this book.

The public reaction to *Dynamics of Neighborhood Change* signals the danger in oversimplifying neighborhood trends into one simple continuum. In 1975 HUD commissioned the Real Estate Research Corporation to publicize its five-stage theory of decline in a set of regional workshops. Anthony Downs, as keynoter in these workshops, advanced the notion that intervention early in the process of decline, Stages 2 or 3, was more cost-effective than later, in States 4 or 5. To make this point, Downs used the analogy of triage—assisting only those battle victims who have a chance of surviving—unaware of ambiguities in applying the analogy to neighborhoods. Not only was it unclear whether he intended to imply that some neighborhood residents or some portions of the stock were beyond assistance, but more significantly, triage glossed over the underlying conflict between equity and effectiveness: helping all a little bit, or doing the "right" thing for a few and worrying about the rest later. The resulting uproar against triage has not resolved any of the dilemmas surrounding appropriate interventions. Rather, it has made policymakers more reluctant to classify neighborhoods publicly. Nevertheless, the underlying point that neighborhood context makes a difference was forcefully made.

THE IMPORTANCE OF NEIGHBORHOODS

The need to monitor and analyze neighborhoods is best illustrated by considering the housing problem—how to provide everyone with a decent home in a suitable living environment as promised by the

1949 Housing Act. It is clearer now that building 26 million new units, as the Kaiser Commission recommended, will not solve the problem. It is not that simple. To develop any policies regarding housing needs and priorities, *households*, *housing units*, and *neighborhoods* must be differentiated. That is, one must distinguish between people, place, and context. Leaving them tangled together and calling it all housing confuses matters.

Households have various associated characteristics such as the size of the household, the age and race of the head, the amount of income being spent for housing, and the percentage being spent. (The available income is less important.) It is productive to differentiate among many of these aspects. For example, single elderly individuals are quite different in their housing needs from single welfare mothers with four teenage boys.

Housing units also have their associated characteristics. Heading the list are the size, condition, location, and cost of units in the stock. Age is becoming less important as trend setters prefer quality, older housing. Most would agree that past indicators, like lack of plumbing facilities, now fail to adequately describe substandard conditions.

The *neighborhood* is a factor. While most households tend to find appropriate housing units on their own, public concern focuses on mismatches. The poor family that pays too much for substandard quarters, the minority family excluded on the basis of race, the widow on a pension who will be displaced because gentrification is inflating her rent, tenants who do not wish to become owners of their units when converted to condominiums—there are an infinite number of these mismatches between particular households and their housing units.

The challenge is to discover some inspired ways of describing the mismatches that capture them in the public mind, are useful for measuring progress, and at the same time will remain salient for 1980 and 1990. Ideally, the way needs are described, or the mismatches defined, should suggest the appropriate kind of program response. The neighborhood context makes the most critical difference.

Instead of simply asking if a unit is too dilapidated, too costly, or in too unsuitable a neighborhood, housing matches should be considered in light of neighborhood dynamics. This will help to determine priorities and appropriate strategies and will point out why neighborhoods are important.

Substandard units, even ones that were abandoned, sometimes are restored as a new market dynamic sweeps across a neighborhood. This reveals an important aspect that was missing in past discussions of the housing problem, *neighborhood context*.

The people who own homes as well as the renters are generally motivated to correct inadequacies if they can and if it makes sense to them. While the syndrome of disinvestment and abandonment is real, motivation provided by the neighborhood context is a more important factor than household income in predicting the future condition of the units.

To understand better these improvement dynamics, Boston, for example, found it useful to differentiate among *homes* (which include one- to four-unit dwellings and condominiums), *apartments* (multifamily structures held by investor owners who are motivated by profit), and *projects* (which are the Section 221(d)(3) and 236 developments and housing projects under public assistance).

In apartments, which comprise one-third of the stock in cities like Boston, the traditional economic incentives have often eroded or become obscured by red tape. In weaker neighborhoods ownership is shifting to irresponsible or inexperienced owners because the economic motivation to maintain properly is no longer there. In strong neighborhoods, efforts to convert to condominiums and reap gains from speculation are on the increase. Owner motivation, provided by neighborhood context, turns out to be a key factor in determining the future.

Units in housing projects and HUD-assisted developments (about one-sixth of Boston's stock) are sometimes in a deplorable state. HUD has quietly temporized by introducing substantial Section 8 subsidies to ameliorate the situation in some projects, while others are sliding back into HUD possession through foreclosure. The very presence of such troubled projects can make all involved in the surrounding neighborhood more discouraged about its future.

Viewing this over time, an interesting dynamic emerges. In stable neighborhoods housing is generally maintained, but elsewhere it is either being disinvested or speculated upon. The stigma or status conferred on living in a particular neighborhood distorts how resources are allocated. People are now willing to pay much more than average to live in what is considered the right neighborhoods.

Whether people put their extra dollars into their homes rather than move to a better address is a function of the neighborhood context. This, even more than available income, increasingly determines whether housing is going to improve or be maintained. Dwellings that house the elderly in a good area cost very little to maintain, while even a fortune cannot prevent deterioration in some stigmatized environments.

The neighborhood context has a strong influence on the behavior of all the housing participants and in turn sharply influences market values. Considering neighborhood context forces policymakers to deal with the perceptions of the residents and all the other interests who tie into the neighborhood—lenders, people who handle buying and selling, and so forth.

Stable neighborhoods, where demand is steady and predictable, represent a comparatively efficient allocation of resources. Declining neighborhoods are at one extreme where disinvestment is rampant and deterioration far more rapid than under traditional filtration. Here housing is no longer maintained. This represents a serious erosion of the capital stock, imposing a large hidden future cost to society. The red-lining issue reflects attempts to devise symptomatic corrections for this fundamental problem.

Rising neighborhoods have now appeared at the other extreme. These involve gentrification, condominium conversions, reinvestment/displacement, or speculation. If there were not so many people desiring housing in these neighborhoods, it would be available at a more reasonable purchase price or at lower rentals.

The perennial debate about rigorously defining a neighborhood is largely a red herring even while neighborhood context is critical. "Neighborhood" here simply refers to any urban area that serves as an arena, marketplace, or crossroads for the behavior of many people in an increasing number of roles: residents, buyers, sellers, brokers, appraisers, lenders, investors, and so on. Each individually defines the neighborhood's geographic extent, and whether these fully coincide is not important to the argument. As is shown below, the data currently available for developing a neighborhood theory limit what can be understood.

As national housing demand tightens in the future, deflecting young households to occupied urban areas, neighborhood context will become even more critical. However, the return of demand to some disinvested urban neighborhoods will also make the need to differentiate neighborhoods more evident, promising to improve understanding of the underlying dynamics, and to generate more cost-effective programs. It is cheaper to match households with their appropriate units within an understanding of forces that can complement their own efforts than to continue to commit Section 8 assistance in the current pattern, helping only a few of the households in need wherever the market is at extremes.

Summary

Past definitions of the housing problem in terms of unit conditions and household income are inadequate. Even though increased understanding of neighborhood context will not solve everything, it is a liberating step forward that will redirect research toward the development of better tools, providing more influence over housing markets.

Whether a substandard unit is located in a context of disinvestment or in a rising housing market should indicate different policy treatments. Thus the most important neighborhood data are those that provide clues to these different motivating climates. Changes in attitudes and perceptions are at least as important as traditional data on housing conditions and household incomes.

At this early stage of understanding neighborhood evolution, several principles already emerge that can guide further data gathering and analysis. Monitoring perceived change should be made a primary goal of data collection, even though this kind of data is much more difficult to obtain. Such change is best detected through the collection of consistent data in a time series. Repeating one simple count several years later is much more useful than two sophisticated but independent counts of the housing stock several years apart, one structure-based, the other unit-based. Monitoring *changes* in the vacancy rate or the ownership turnover rate leads to more important clues to perceived change than knowing the actual rates.

In mathematical terms, first and second derivatives are more important than absolute numbers. For example, exploring how the rates of change diverge in similar neighborhoods, or how the rates of change themselves alter over time—these are the most useful data for coming to understand neighborhood evolution and developing constructive interventions.

Monitoring the interface between buyers and sellers is the best proxy for neighborhood change. How many are trying to sell? Are there more or less than a year ago? How many are seeking to buy? How do shifting trends in occupations of buyers and sellers at this market interface compare to the city norm? While these are extremely difficult data to obtain rigorously and consistently, obtaining them focuses the data search.

PROPOSING A TWO-DIMENSIONAL CONCEPTUAL FRAMEWORK FOR NEIGHBORHOOD CLASSIFICATION

A single continuum of decline arose logically from the concepts of housing filtration, or the appraisers' theories of housing age, condition, and obsolescence going hand in hand. However, this no longer appears to fit. Physically similar structures built in different neighborhoods of the same city at the same time can today be found in very different market dynamics. One in a declining market may be experiencing disinvestment while another in a rising market may be experiencing gentrification.

Figure 3—1 stresses that the policy aim for any neighborhood, regardless of condition, should be to steer between market extremes on either side. Policymakers must combine their traditional sensitivity to physical housing conditions with a new awareness of neighborhood market perceptions. This means public policy must become sensitive and countervailing to neighborhood dynamics, increasing demand where it is weak and areas are declining, and cooling it where markets are rising, resulting in dislocation and speculation.

It is critical to separate objective housing conditions from subjective expectations of neighborhood future and from outside forces that shape actual housing market behavior. This further specifies the type of data most useful for monitoring and analyzing neighborhood change. Figure 3—2 shows the resulting conceptual framework.

Housing condition data are essential to determine where and by how much local situations fall short of publicly accepted standards. In effect, they indicate the cost gap that must be closed in order for everyone to have a decent home. Although necessary, condition data are insufficient to determine how that gap can best be permanently bridged (Goetze, 1976).

The cost of maintaining and upgrading is a function of condition; but the incentive to do so depends in many cases on the strength of housing demand and the change in market value resulting from upgrading. The advantage of a matrix approach is that it differentiates declining from revitalizing dynamics in neighborhoods with similar physical conditions. They are not mirror images, and the different dynamics will become increasingly important as more households reconsider city living.

One would expect good housing conditions and strong neighborhood markets, and poor conditions and weak markets, to go together. To a large degree they do. However, *where they do not is of particular interest to the policymakers.* Wherever there is only a mixed market for good housing or a strong market for mediocre structures requires particular vigilance. An excessively strong market is suboptimal, even for good condition housing, because the incentive for proper maintenance erodes in markets where virtually anything can be sold or rented.

Generally, housing can be expected to lie along the dotted line in Figure 3—2. In cities with strong overall housing demand, actual distribution of the stock will shift toward the left, and in cities with weak demand the distribution shifts toward the right.

Despite its importance, market strength is difficult to measure. Further, the actual balance between households wishing to enter, remain, or leave a neighborhood may not be as important as the

Figure 3–1. Golden Mean Diagram

Neighborhood Market Types	Rising (Gentrifying) ++	Stable Or Ideal	Declining (Disinvesting) −
Symptoms Indicators (or Causes?)	• Excess demand • Price inflation (real or anticipated) • Speculation • Strong press image • Inmigration of higher class • Investment purchases • Conversion of marginal space into more dwellings	G O L D E N	• Excess supply • Uncertainty in property values • "Red-lining" • Negative press image • Departure of the able • Discretionary sales • Increase in low down payment and/or government insured lending • Increase in absentee ownership • Rising tax delinquency • Property abandonment
Corrective Remedies	• Dampen outside demand • Assist disadvantaged to remain • Enforce code • Prevent illegal conversions • Reassess only upon sale • Control rents if necessary • Construct additional housing	M E A N	• Boost neighborhood image • Value insurance for resident owners • Improve jobs and income without stigma • Support NHS if requested • Demolish excess housing (or mothball) • Land bank vacant lots until stable

Source: Goetze (1977).

Figure 3-2. Universal Neighborhood Classification Matrix

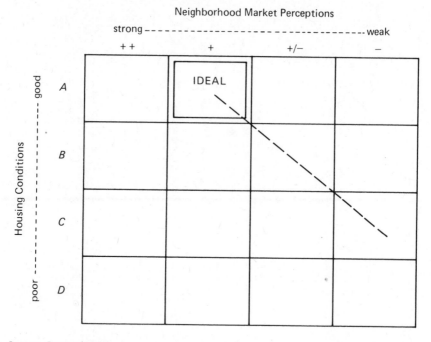

Source: Goetze (1976).

balance perceived by the key participants in the housing process. Discovering indicators of this aggregate perception is the goal.

Status and the expression of one's position in the social order play a powerful role. Within a neighborhood, turnover occurs as new households replace departing ones. The tenor of the neighborhood— declining, revitalizing, gentrifying, or stable—is set by the interplay between indigenous residents and newcomers and, in particular, by the way they perceive each other's status. When vacancies are filled by "more of the same households," likely to be younger but from the same roots, residents generally regard this as "normal" or "stable." However, as different lifestyles enter, even in very small numbers, reactions occur. The more threatening this difference is perceived by the residents, the more extreme their reaction. Communes, welfare dependent households, working class minorities professional households, or minority professionals—each makes its own waves among the resident population.

If neighborhood residents see a significant difference between newcomers and themselves, some alter their investment decisions regarding maintenance and upgrading while others will even reexamine whether to move or stay. Research in Boston reveals that a remarkably small number of newcomers can set off such neighborhood dynamics. When the media detect and broadcast this phobia about newcomers, the message becomes more real than reality, and a self-fulfilling trend may be initiated. It then becomes crucially important whether buyers match sellers or an excess of one over the other develops. Too many sellers indicates declining neighborhood confidence; too many buyers can lead to speculation or "flipping"— buying for resale at profit. When a neighborhood first runs short of normal replacement buyers, that is, when the stream of households that have been coming in the past dwindles, the stage is set for potential change.

Building Neighborhood Confidence (Goetze, 1976) details this dynamic process, furnishes illustrations, and concludes that the two dimensions in Figure 3—2—housing condition and market perception—provide the best basis for a universal neighborhood classification framework. Any system that contains so many conflicting perceptions can only approximate reality since various participants actually see things differently at the same time. But such a matrix allows the important differentiations to be made. For example, in a stable neighborhood of elderly homeowners, housing may be filtering downward in condition from B+ to C+ because the homeowners are undermaintaining, while block-busting may take another B+ neighborhood directly to B− . Conversely, young professionals entering a C− neighborhood could, by their presence alone without any real renovation, make it a C+ revival neighborhood, which then gentrifies through turnover and reinvestment in the individual units to A++. A C++ neighborhood is prone to displacement, while a C− neighborhood is prone to arson. Figure 3—3 shows these dynamics on the classification framework.

Before exploring how such a neighborhood classification system can be made operational, it is important to mention some factors constraining its development in spite of its benefits.

FACTORS DISCOURAGING
NEIGHBORHOOD MONITORING
AND ANALYSIS

While there is often agreement that appropriate neighborhood policies cannot be developed without some neighborhood classification system, public officials at all levels appear reluctant to proceed for three important reasons. First, *they fear that classification is self-fulfilling.* They are afraid that by explicitly identifying a dynamic,

Figure 3–3.   The Matrix of Housing Dynamics

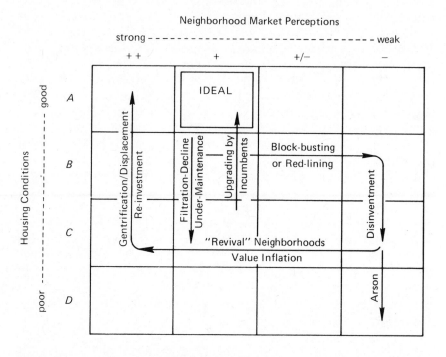

the planners would trigger more dysfunctional behavior in investors, lenders, and even residents by influencing decisions to move, stay, or upgrade. Certainly bankers who declined to make mortgages in weaker areas, even without any actual red-pencilled maps, have been accused of "red-lining," which some claim causes deterioration, loss of confidence, and disinvestment. While self-fulfilling prophecies are a serious concern, the market responds to media sensations. The market often erratically makes judgments about neighborhood dynamics, many of which are more negative than actual circumstances warrant. That is because outside investors, appraisers, and lenders are conservative and must allow for potential negative dynamics as they commit the resources of others.

Second, *officials fear resident reaction.* Some residents are reluctant to face up to a changed dynamic or are adamant but unrealistic about the public sector role. People do not wish to hear that they live in a neighborhood where negative dynamics are continuing. For these people, hearing the news officially from a government that should remedy the situation provokes antagonism. Residents easily recognize when classification is used only to determine where to invest scarce resources. The concept of triage—concentrating scarce assistance on neighborhoods where it can make the most difference— has developed a strong emotional charge because triage implies abandoning the most distressed neighborhoods or the neediest households. Obviously the government cannot identify the neediest only to turn its back on them.

The third reason is more personal. *Neighborhood indicators would improve accountability*. Rather than permitting each staff member to feel he was doing all he could, neighborhood monitoring might reveal the ineffectuality of some endeavors or force program cutbacks.

There are many benefits in classifying neighborhoods by their dynamics. Careful neighborhood analysis offers the promise of raising planning theory to the point where the consequences of intervention become better understood and more predictable. However, the above objections are so serious within the context of our political system that nonpolitical organizations are best equipped to classify neighborhoods and survive the heat that classification is likely to generate among residents as well as public officials. The next section describes progress being made on this frontier.

MUNICIPAL NEIGHBORHOOD CLASSIFICATION SYSTEMS

Specifications were developed above for data that would be useful in monitoring and analyzing neighborhood changes: the data would be consistently gathered information suitable for developing time series of changes as well as for detecting differential rates of change among various neighborhoods. Before examining the most suitable data currently available in light of these requirements, it is useful to review a few municipal neighborhood classification efforts. Their description here is intended to be neither exhaustive nor complete; they are only presented to be reviewed in light of the criteria developed in the previous section.

A number of cities have recently developed special classification systems for targeting discretionary assistance such as Community Development Block Grants (CDBG), but these are not sensitive enough for neighborhood monitoring or analysis. They typically deal with gross factors and information several years old rather than focusing on net changes, year by year. In the past, when federal programs required targeting, U.S. census data were judged adequate for the selection of appropriate neighborhoods as, for example, in designating federally assisted code enforcement (FACE) program areas. However, when such targeting decisions were shifted to local jurisdictions, municipalities felt a greater need to justify the selection of particular areas for assistance. Also, the 1970 census data were becoming out of date. As a result, municipalities sought to include such factors in the data as the presence of strong neighborhood associations or more detailed and current housing condition information. Many urban community development administrations developed and publicly debated their own priority systems so that they could better defend themselves when criticized by residents in areas not given priority.

These systems are usually either based on exogenous assumptions regarding appropriate areas for intervention (e.g., in early stages of decline, before deterioration has seriously advanced) or have been designed as a screen for defending *a priori* selections (e.g., where a particularly important political constituency resides). Ambiguities in their purpose are seldom addressed. These systems tend to justify priorities rather than serve as a guide. An analogous process is the way northeastern cities lobbied to revise the CDBG allocation formula in the wake of "hold-harmless" so that age of housing stock, which would increase their share, became a more significant determinant of their entitlement.

However, a number of cities developed multipurpose data systems—a sort of "stew" of all available information. The nature of the stew is a function of the available data and the creativity and intentions of the local "cooks." Generally they assume a linear progression of neighborhood change, perhaps because these municipalities engaged consultants like the Real Estate Research Corporation, which produced *Dynamics of Change* for HUD in 1975, or the R.L. Polk Company which provides urban statistical data as an offshoot of its annual household and business directories in many major cities. Frequently sales data, mortgage data, crime, or school data were also factored in. Evaluating the effectiveness of public interventions or even challenging assumptions about how the housing market works and responds to interventions was not a primary purpose of these classification systems because they were created by action-oriented administrations, not evaluators.

Memphis developed a very complex but publicly open system involving a host of indicators to assist in targeting CDBG funds into intermediate areas with effective neighborhood organizations. This information system in effect informs areas they must become organized to qualify for aid. Technical assistance is even available for this purpose.

Indianapolis and Milwaukee appear to have developed particularly elaborate systems for typing areas. In Indianapolis each of five types is correlated to appropriate housing assistance, although a court suit involving metropolitan school desegregation currently suspends all housing actions. In Milwaukee a system was developed to differentiate six types of areas, called Relative Residential Status (RRS). The typology separates out unique, primarily multifamily areas, then clusters similar or usually matched household and housing stock types together and then attempts to rank residential status from top to bottom (healthy market, highest assessed values and rate of owner occupancy, lowest vacancy rate). Community suspicions regarding the purposes of the RRS ranking system run high. Residents took issue with a phrase in RRS Area IV, "market beginning to falter," and forced its retraction. One neighborhood, River West, has challenged the system. This has resulted in designation of a seventh type, "Special Study Area," or as residents put it, "specially ornery."

Prince George's County, a partially built-up urban country flanking the District of Columbia on the east, has developed a remarkably explicit system for classifying the dynamics within its municipalities. It states current conditions and anticipated future dynamic in each, for example, fair condition, continuing deterioration. The inclusion of these ratings in the county CDBG application is in sharp contrast to the usual euphemisms in which most CDBG applicants discuss their declining areas. Perhaps the professionals in this urban county administration can avoid political heat by relating directly to their counterparts within the county but are buffered from the actual citizens. Many urban municipalities seem to fear that neighborhood classification would raise unpleasant reactions among organized constituencies.

Some cities, like Portland, Oregon, have already developed a reputation for having a Neighborhood Management Information System when they as yet have little more than a promising concept paper within the Department of Commerce/Cities Program. Here a very elaborate multipurpose approach is in its early, and probably over-optimistic, design stage.

Publications by individuals in Pittsburgh (Ahlbrandt, 1977), Portland (Lipton, 1977), or Boston (Goetze, 1976) often have much to offer, but they frequently create the impression that local decision-makers are guided by some actual information system.

In the Pittsburgh Neighborhood Atlas Project an alliance of social scientists and neighborhood leaders set out, with city support, to develop economic, demographic, and quality of life indicators, including citizen perceptions on attitudes for each neighborhood. Delineating the resulting seventy-eight neighborhoods to obtain consensus without geographic overlaps was a significant achievement in itself. Each neighborhood now has its boundaries and an atlas, both in print and in accessible computer form, containing the following data:

1. Neighborhood description (acres, distance from downtown);
2. Neighborhood map depicting actual street boundaries;
3. Neighborhood satisfaction (questions from citizen survey);
4. Neighborhood problems (from the citizen survey);
5. Satisfaction with public services (from the citizen survey);
6. Crime rate;
7. Characteristics of the neighborhood population;
8. Neighborhood income;
9. Public assistance data;
10. Housing characteristics;
11. Real estate and mortgage loan data; and
12. Voter registration.

This achievement has not yet been developed into a time series, but it offers comparisons between neighborhoods at the same point in time. While the process of defining neighborhoods is instructive, it is difficult to anticipate how the atlas will respond to natural population shifts.

Boston disseminates annual profiles on its twenty-two planning districts. It has already shifted its 1970 districts more than once, pointing out the research dilemma of whether to stick with population or geography. For example, Roxbury, the principal black district, has been shifted south, outward from the central business district. While this allows Boston to continue to relate its assistance efforts explicitly to each neighborhood constituency, it means information must be maintained in many smaller building blocks no larger than census tracts, which are shifted from district to district over time.

The Department of Commerce appears to be designing the 1980 census compilations around the concept of neighborhoods, perhaps inspired by the Pittsburgh atlas project, or the census subtotals by neighborhood that Boston developed for itself from the 1970 data years ago. The dilemma of how best to shift districts is not explicitly debated in the Commerce/Cities project.

Boston appears to be one of the few cities to have begun systematically to repeat attitude sampling so that a time series of changing neighborhood perceptions becomes available; but even here the data are costly, cumbersome, and fragmentary.

This brief review of municipal neighborhood classification systems suggests that few are well suited to monitoring or analyzing changing dynamics because they are not based on annual time series data. While they can corroborate gross trends, they cannot detect net changes. None appear sensitive enough or designed to identify the precise causes of change, particularly for any analysis that attempts comparisons between similar neighborhoods in different jurisdictions. For lack of operational standards, similar neighborhoods cannot yet even be rigorously identified through these local efforts.

THE COMMUNITY ANALYSIS MODEL

An MIT group, headed by David L. Birch, has developed a reputation for leadership in modelling neighborhood change; but in this model, promise is especially difficult to separate from achievements. Since the model has only been built or fitted to six cities and access to it is difficult to obtain, one can only judge it by what the authors have written. Their writings appear promotional rather than focused on what they have already learned about neighborhood change.

Essentially the model tracks a large number of changes on an annual basis, pointing out that it follows the behavior of participants (households, individuals, homeowners, landlords, builders, lenders, insurers, employers, etc.) making decisions within certain determinants. Many of the participants are stratified by age, ethnicity or race, and education, but it is not clear how the authors decided to limit differentiations. Figure 3−4 suggests the level of specificity of the model and Figure 3−5 shows its basic structure. It is not easy to determine its usefulness to neighborhood monitoring and analysis, but it seems like technological overkill—like trying to develop a computerized robot to obtain a good cup of coffee.

Figure 3–4.   Sample of Roles in the MIT Community Analysis Model

Role	*Decision*	*Stratification*	*Major Determinants*
Homeowner	Setting selling price of home	Age by Economic class/Race by Education by Price of home	Potential demand relative to available units
	Investing in home maintenance		Characteristics of homeowner (e.g., housing preferences) Characteristics of housing unit (e.g., age of unit) Characteristics of neighborhood (e.g., average housing condition)
Landlord	Setting rent levels on apartments	Rent level of apartments	Potential demand relative to available units
	Investing or disinvesting in maintenance for apartments (including abandoning apartments)		Characteristics of tenants (e.g., age, education, ethnicity) Characteristics of apartment (e.g., age of unit) Characteristics of neighborhood (e.g., ethnic composition)

Builder		
Constructing single-family homes under contract	Contract vs. Speculative Type of unit (tenure and price)	Vacancy rate in submarket and region Availability of suitable vacant land Availability of credit
Constructing apartments under contract		Absorption rate in submarket Excess demand in submarket Vacancy rate in submarket and region Zoning restrictions Availability of suitable vacant land Availability of credit

Source: David L. Birch et al., "The Community Analysis Model; An Overview," Joint Center for Urban Studies, MIT and Harvard, March 1977.

Figure 3–5.   The MIT Community Analysis Model

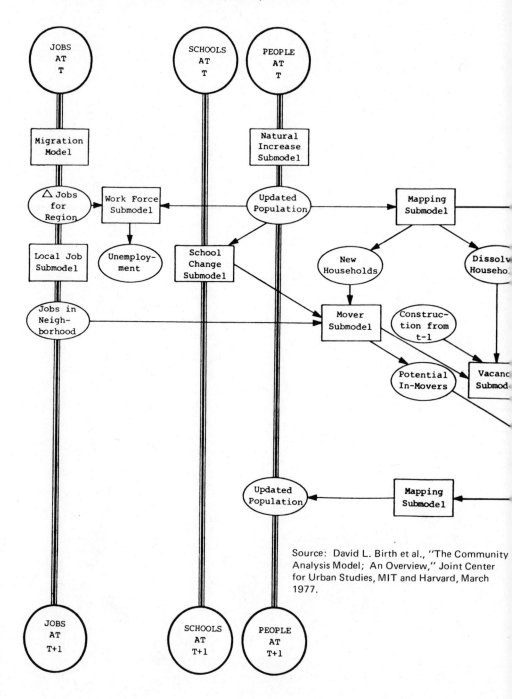

Source: David L. Birth et al., "The Community Analysis Model; An Overview," Joint Center for Urban Studies, MIT and Harvard, March 1977.

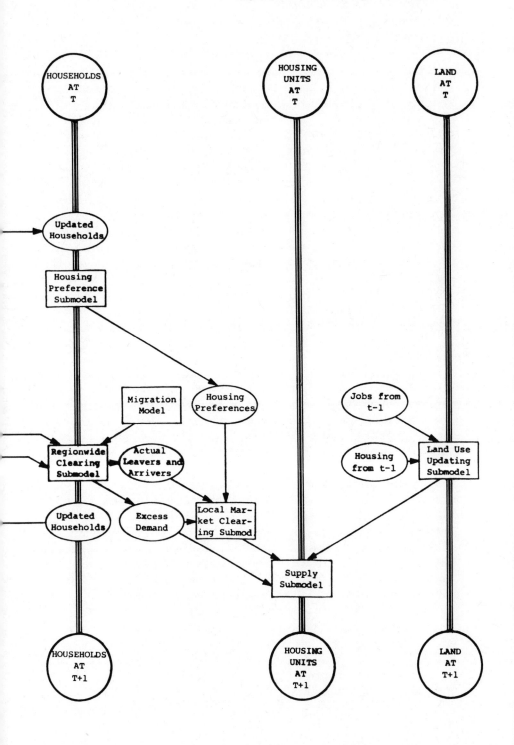

BUILDING MORE BROADLY
ON AVAILABLE DATA

Ironically the most promising approach for monitoring neighborhood change systematically has been available but ignored for some time. A number of private firms maintain annual household directories. The best known, widespread and consistent system for developing a time series is *Profiles of Change*. The R.L. Polk Company annually sends out field enumerators to inventory every household and business establishment in over 300 major U.S. cities—and it continues to do this today, nearly a decade after the U.S. census resorted to mailing its questionnaires. While critics can spot many shortcomings in Polk's method (touched on below), it is the only available and independent annual census of appropriate statistics that has remained consistent over time. It even appears to be relatively consistent across all the covered jurisdictions. That alone puts it ahead of anything else.

Figure 3—6 shows the information contained in the annual Street Directory. Even more useful, the data are electronically stored and retrievable at the dwelling unit level, much like a telephone directory, but one that can be organized by address, names, occupations, and so forth.

Whereas the U.S. census aggregates the data into census blocks and tracts to prepare it for print and to provide confidentiality, the Polk data are simply public record information and left at the unit level. The unit basis enables much richer analysis if one has the electronic capability. For example, instead of explicitly requiring a question, "Did you move during the last year?" as the census does, Polk data can answer such questions instantly because this year's tape can be compared with last year's for the same unit.

Anyone who has worked with traditional census data will recall the frustration of dealing in simple cross tabulations. "X percent of the mover households were renters," "Y percent of the mover households had incomes below $5000"—how many of the movers were both renters *and* had low income is unknown. They may have been largely one and the same or, then again, they may mostly have been independent. False inferences about revitalization are often made at this point, as observers interpret census-type tabulations through incorrect assumptions, for example, expecting filtration to reverse itself. If higher income homeowners move out first during filtration (true), they will come back last in reverse filtration (false). Boston data show this is erroneous. In fact, the first pioneer households are quite unconventional yet invisible in traditional statistics. In Polk

Figure 3-6. Street Directory, R.L. Polk Co.

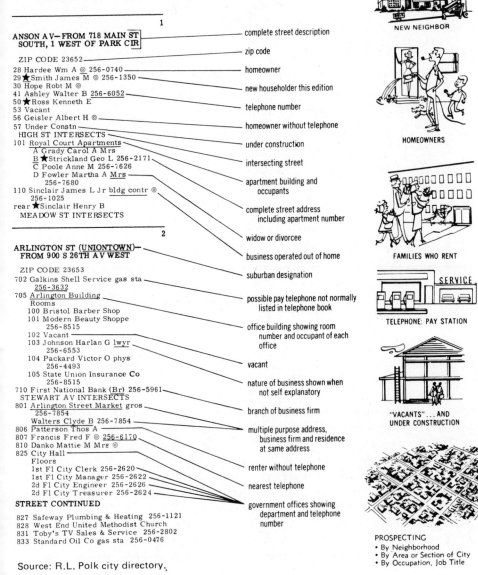

STREET DIRECTORY
GREEN PAGES

◎ HOMEOWNER SYMBOL   ★ NEW NEIGHBOR SYMBOL

1

ANSON AV—FROM 718 MAIN ST ──── complete street description
SOUTH, 1 WEST OF PARK CIR

ZIP CODE 23652 ──── zip code

28 Hardee Wm A ◎ 256-0740 ──── homeowner
29 ★Smith James M ◎ 256-1350 ──── new householder this edition
30 Hope Robt M ◎
41 Ashley Walter B 256-6052 ──── telephone number
50 ★Ross Kenneth E
53 Vacant
56 Geisler Albert H ◎ ──── homeowner without telephone
57 Under Constn ──── under construction
HIGH ST INTERSECTS ──── intersecting street
101 Royal Court Apartments ──── apartment building and occupants
    A Grady Carol A Mrs
    B ★Strickland Geo L 256-2171
    C Poole Anne M 256-7626
    D Fowler Martha A Mrs ──── complete street address including apartment number
      256-7680
110 Sinclair James L Jr bldg contr ◎
    256-1025
rear ★Sinclair Henry B
    MEADOW ST INTERSECTS

2

ARLINGTON ST (UNIONTOWN)— ──── widow or divorcee
FROM 900 S 26TH AV WEST ──── business operated out of home

ZIP CODE 23653 ──── suburban designation
702 Galkins Shell Service gas sta
    256-3632 ──── possible pay telephone not normally listed in telephone book
705 Arlington Building
    Rooms
    100 Bristol Barber Shop
    101 Modern Beauty Shoppe ──── office building showing room number and occupant of each office
      256-8515
    102 Vacant ──── vacant
    103 Johnson Harlan G lwyr
      256-6553
    104 Packard Victor O phys ──── nature of business shown when not self explanatory
      256-4493
    105 State Union Insurance Co
      256-8515
710 First National Bank (Br) 256-5961 ──── branch of business firm
    STEWART AV INTERSECTS
801 Arlington Street Market gros
    256-7854
    Walters Clyde B 256-7854 ──── multiple purpose address, business firm and residence at same address
806 Patterson Thos A
807 Francis Fred F ◎ 256-6170
810 Danko Mattie M Mrs ◎ ──── renter without telephone
825 City Hall
    Floors
    1st Fl City Clerk 256-2620 ──── nearest telephone
    1st Fl City Manager 256-2622
    2d Fl City Engineer 256-2626
    2d Fl City Treasurer 256-2624
STREET CONTINUED ──── government offices showing department and telephone number

827 Safeway Plumbing & Heating 256-1121
828 West End United Methodist Church
831 Toby's TV Sales & Service 256-2802
833 Standard Oil Co gas sta 256-0476

Source: R.L. Polk city directory.

NEW NEIGHBOR

HOMEOWNERS

FAMILIES WHO RENT

SERVICE

TELEPHONE: PAY STATION

"VACANTS"... AND UNDER CONSTRUCTION

PROSPECTING
• By Neighborhood
• By Area or Section of City
• By Occupation, Job Title

data one can look for the individual pioneer households by their peculiar characteristics.

Because the Polk data are so basic, that is, based on appropriate elements, much more sophisticated analysis becomes possible. In fact the Polk urban statistical division already has devised a system of Neighborhood Situation Ratings (NSRs) at the census tract level, based on the combination of over a dozen factors their annual surveys collect and put on data tapes. For each condition (A through D) each census tract is ranked relative to all others in the same city according to a composite of eight factors that appear to be reliable proxies:

- Residential units recently vacated or newly completed;
- Residential units found vacant at each of two directory canvasses (usually an indicator of housing deterioration or even abandonment);
- Vacant commercial units;
- Occupied housing units with a change of household (high mobility rates frequently indicate demographic instability);
- Jobless heads of household;
- Female heads of household with children;
- Low income households;
- Household money income.

It is important to note that the condition rating indicates only the rank or position of a tract in relation to all other tracts in the city or city-wide averages and, as such, does not measure current conditions in absolute terms.

All the census tracts are then placed into four categories: top quartile, A; upper-middle, B; lower middle, C; and bottom quartile, D. Map 3-1 shows a typical city in this system.

To arrive at neighborhood change ratings, twelve factors from two consecutive enumerations are combined to reveal shifts over time. This provides only a proxy for market perception, but its easy availability compensates for its approximate fit. The Polk staff has devised a complex weighting function to combine all these factors into one index of change, which it has recently computerized. Table 3-1 shows how these variables are conceptually related.

This indexing as currently constituted is absolute. Each neighborhood develops a score that causes it to be assigned to one of four categories called strongly positive, ++; moderately positive, +; nega-

Map 3–1. Current Status Ratings

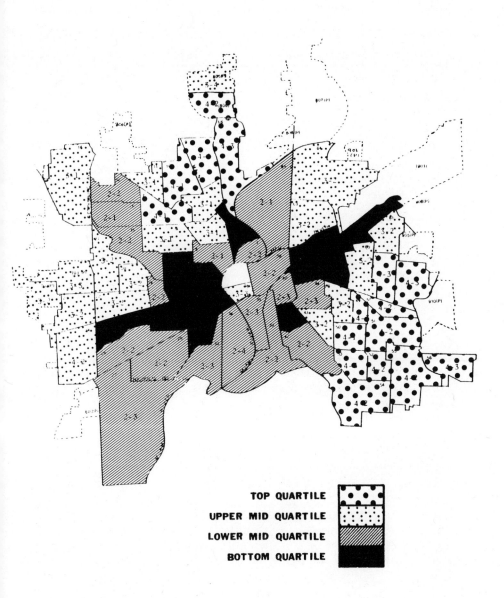

TOP QUARTILE

UPPER MID QUARTILE

LOWER MID QUARTILE

BOTTOM QUARTILE

Source: Developed from R.L. Polk Co., time series data.

Table 3–1. **Factors Combined for Computing Index of Annual Change**

Direction of Change	Indicator	Direction of Change	Indicator
Increase ⟶	Positive	Increase ⟶	Negative
Decrease ⟶	Negative	Decrease ⟶	Positive

• Housing units	• Vacancies in existing housing units
• Households	
• Business firms	• Vacant commercial units
• Households with children	• Female heads of household with children
• Owners	
• Household money income	• Jobless heads of household
• Professional and managerial household heads	• Lower income households

Source: R.L. Polk and Co., Urban Statistical Division.

tive or mixed, +/−; and strongly negative, −. Thus, in a strong city a larger number of neighborhoods may be positive while in a weaker city, more neighborhoods may be mixed and negative. To confine relative or quartile rankings to conditions, as Polk has done, seems appropriate.

As the reader probably noticed, the Polk data enable planners to identify where neighborhoods fit on the Classification Matrix, Figure 3–2 (see pages 36 and 38).

Map 3–2 shows the same city in dynamic terms. It reveals new aspects like negative trends in the northwest and positive trends in the southwest.

For ease of communication Map 3–2 can be split apart to focus on the dynamics around particular housing conditions. For example, Map 3–3 shows only bottom quartile (D-condition) areas, revealing sharply varying dynamics. Without such data planners would be prone to see these neighborhoods simply in the bottom quartile and stop at that.

Map 3–4, lower mid-quartile (C-condition) areas, reveals positive trends in the southwest, suggesting that reinvestment/displacement concerns may soon become appropriate, while strongly negative trends northeast of the CBD might soon require an arson alert.

Maps 3–5 and 3–6, for the better-than-average neighborhoods, are similar, again revealing the various dynamics occurring beneath the surface.

The potential value and usefulness of these data are far-reaching. Since Polk carries data on business firms along with households,

Map 3—2. Neighborhood Change Ratings

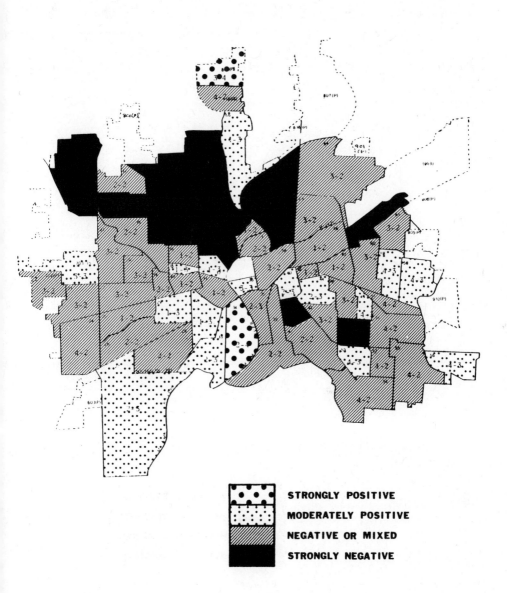

STRONGLY POSITIVE
MODERATELY POSITIVE
NEGATIVE OR MIXED
STRONGLY NEGATIVE

Source: Developed from R.L. Polk Co., time series data.

Map 3–3. Bottom Quartile Areas: Change Ratings

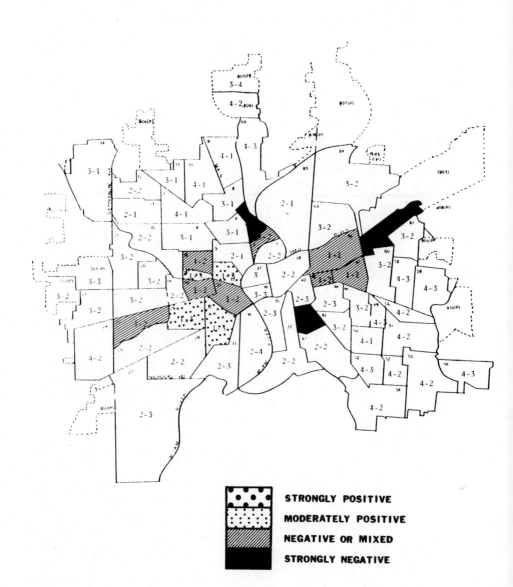

	STRONGLY POSITIVE
	MODERATELY POSITIVE
	NEGATIVE OR MIXED
	STRONGLY NEGATIVE

Source: Developed from R.L. Polk Co., time series data.

Map 3—4. Lower Mid-Quartile Areas: Change Ratings

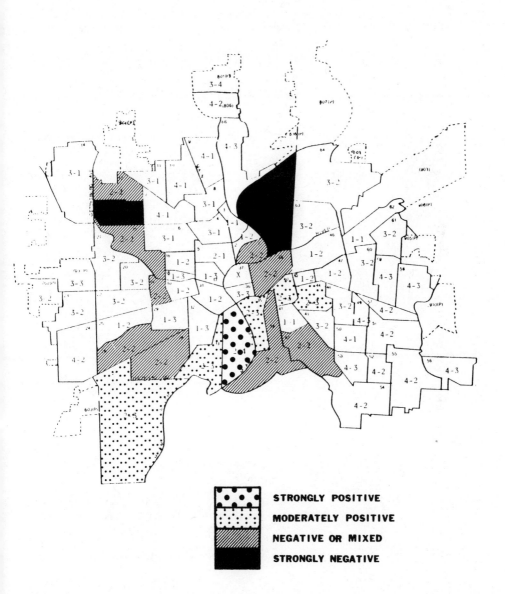

STRONGLY POSITIVE

MODERATELY POSITIVE

NEGATIVE OR MIXED

STRONGLY NEGATIVE

Source: Developed from R.L. Polk Co., time series data.

Map 3–5.   Upper Mid-Quartile Areas: Change Ratings

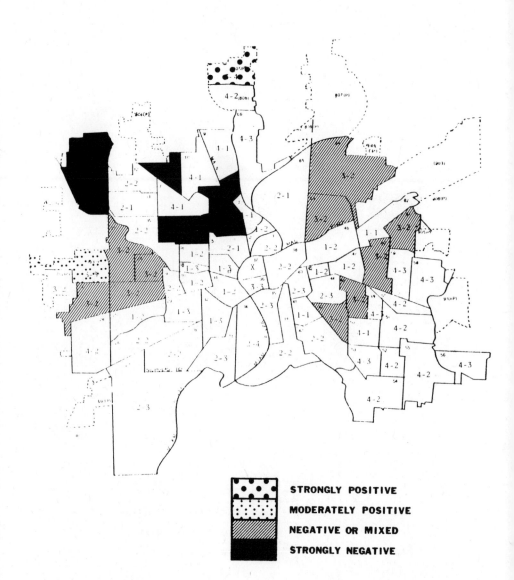

STRONGLY POSITIVE

MODERATELY POSITIVE

NEGATIVE OR MIXED

STRONGLY NEGATIVE

Source: Developed from R.L. Polk Co., time series data.

Map 3–6. Top Quartile Areas: Change Ratings

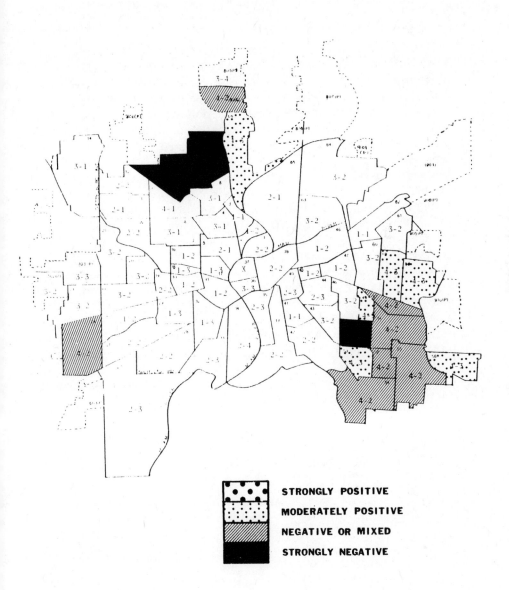

STRONGLY POSITIVE

MODERATELY POSITIVE

NEGATIVE OR MIXED

STRONGLY NEGATIVE

Source: Developed from R.L. Polk Co., time series data.

some previously inconceivable micro-analyses become possible. How do shifts from resident to absentee ownership relate to business turnover? In cities like Boston, where the history of changing credit availability is also known, one could determine which actions lead and which follow.

Obviously the use of a research and analytical system such as this is more promise than reality for most cities. Fitting such data to the actual dynamics of market strength and perception requires extensive field testing before wide-spread adoption. Even then, field verification will always be essential before any policy actions are taken. Any statistical proxy for intangible perceptions can be too easily distorted by a simple change like completion of a large, new rental housing complex.

Many will be quick to spot other weaknesses in the Polk data. "It isn't 100% accurate." "It doesn't count race." "Two income households aren't identified." "It's terribly cumbersome." "The rating system is negative in its approach." While these criticisms may be true, *year by year changes* are needed, and few reliable measures exist. Having the Polk data is like finding an informative new channel on our television set. While the quality of the picture may not be top-notch, its content makes up for it, as long as the action can be followed. Further research is needed to confirm whether the picture is adequate for tracking the changes, but Polk promises to be an improvement over available alternatives. However, these indicators can only be guides to action and have nowhere near the reliability of blips on a radar screen. Field verification and open discussions of issues with residents and other participants will always remain essential planning functions.

Chapter 4

Laying A New Groundwork

Time series data for tracking neighborhood change only begin to point research in a more fruitful direction. A better understanding of the many forces influencing neighborhoods is needed. This chapter presents an illustrative case study based on research into actual change in Boston, and then explores how more unorthodox research approaches can help increase understanding of neighborhood dynamics.

Traditional urban research techniques, stressing hard data for validation, are poorly suited to the current state of urban knowledge. There is only a limited amount of soft data amid profound conceptual confusion. Coherence, insights, and a guiding theory can spring from emphasizing description, inferring from pathologies, and puzzling about the broader contextual forces shaping neighborhood change. Once promising theories are articulated, the more traditional urban research techniques can be employed for verification.

AN ILLUSTRATIVE CASE OF
NEIGHBORHOOD CHANGE:
JAMAICA PLAIN

The nature and extent of neighborhood changes currently underway are best revealed by an actual case in which the basic neighborhood trend, disinvestment, has been transformed into potential displacement within six years.

Jamaica Plain is a residential neighborhood of one- to three-family frame houses, four miles from the downtown core of Boston, lying between affluent Brookline and Roxbury, Boston's black ghetto. The housing stock is richly varied, ranging from Victorian country homes built by Boston's gentry, to triple-deckers, a structure type that enabled immigrants to become homeowners and to build up equity by renting out the upper floors of their homes. Not only does Jamaica Plain now contain a number of public housing projects, but in several subareas it has a growing Spanish-speaking population.

In the early 1970s residents encountered difficulties in obtaining bank credit for home repairs, and several potential buyers documented the runaround they were given in trying to finance a house— in short, red-lining was present.

Research into the annual rate of homeownership turnover throughout the city between 1969 and 1974 revealed that it ranged between a low of 2.5 percent, which is seen as stagnant, to a high of 25 percent, sustained for only brief periods, which is called block-busting. In Jamaica Plain around 5 percent normally changed hands each year. Thus in a neighborhood of 1,000 structures containing around 2,000 homes, only 50 changed to new owners annually. Yet many of the 2,000 households were more sensitive to newcomers among the 50 replacement buyers than simple arithmetic would suggest. This research also showed that in Jamaica Plain, credit for purchase was often furnished by the seller, whereas in areas not threatened by racial changes such seller credit was rare. (Purchases through installment contracts do not occur in Boston.)

In the early 1970s, brokers and appraisers were communicating a pessimistic view to potential buyers interested in the Jamaica Plain market. Nevertheless, some young pioneers were able to buy houses in good condition. Residents were confused about the future of the area. Some were preoccupied by the few absentee owners buying, others were concerned about encroaching minorities, and a few took the presence of the more educated pioneers as a positive sign.

A coalition of residents and newcomers formed the Jamaica Plain Banking and Mortgage Committee to address red-lining. Prior to the 1974 gubernatorial election they obtained promises from each candidate that he would appoint a sensitive bank commissioner. In 1975, Massachusetts attained mortgage disclosure, and newly appointed Commissioner Greenwalt, the lenders, and some community representatives set up an effective mortgage review board.

In the fall of 1974, a group of graduate students, directed by William Harris at Boston University, initiated a commercial television special focusing on several enthusiastic residents, some of them newcomers. Whether the showing of this up-beat program on prime time in January 1975 coincided with or actually caused a market turn-around cannot be proven, but one of the local real estate brokers remarked soon after, "I don't know how the program did it. I received many new inquiries from good prospects—but many of my listings dried up, so I couldn't show them what I thought I had." The strong influence of television on perception and neighborhood behavior was unexpected.

To coincide with the television special, the Boston Redevelopment Authority (BRA) released an eye-catching poster, in Spanish as well as English depicting the strong points of living in Jamaica Plain. Planners became increasingly aware of how regularly they had stressed abandoned houses, poverty, and neighborhood problems in their efforts to secure more federal funds. How refreshing it was to be up-beat and to focus on the neighborhood's valuable assets!

In 1974, the Little City Hall manager conducted a house-by-house condition survey of a 4,000 unit subarea housing some minorities (Speers, 1978). In early 1978, these same structures were resurveyed. Conditions were still mixed, and 50 percent of the structures had not changed appreciably. But only 8 percent had deteriorated further, while 42 percent had decidedly improved, indicating that reinvestment and upgrading by the residents was quietly going on.

Ownership turnover in the early 1970s was perceived as leading to "problem owners" by real estate actors and some residents; but in 1978 a wide and healthy variety of newcomers was seen. Actual facts on turnover are secondary to these perceptions in shaping resident behavior. Displacement of original residents has not been mentioned as an issue, but media stories may cause people to see it in normal turnover. Perceptions obviously play a more important role here than traditional theory provides.

These fears, perceptions, and expectations of who will live in the area largely determine how homes are maintained. The tone and content of neighborhood coverage by the media caused confidence first to ebb, then to surge. Actual events such as the change in credit availability are secondary or often go unnoticed in the decision to remain, invest, or move, until broadcast by the media.

This leads to insights that challenge past policies. As life becomes more complex, Boston research suggests that more and more people take their cues from the media instead of trusting their own senses. A myriad of individual decisions are involved in maintaining a neighborhood. Brokers, potential buyers, appraisers, lenders, and existing residents are increasingly swayed by media impressions as fewer and fewer people are able to see the way things are going first hand. In marginal neighborhoods it makes a critical difference whether the glass is seen as half empty or half full!

Affordability—the notion that available household income determines housing conditions—has long been a cornerstone of public policy. However, knowledge of the behavior of residents in Jamaica Plain suggests that mobility and media images of the neighborhood are also important determinants of housing conditions. Conditions in Jamaica Plain are improving now because of an attitude change rather than an income change. In areas where residents can easily move, affordability alone no longer governs neighborhood vitality.

Neighborhood confidence is critical to improvement. A study in 1973 of the Federally Assisted Code Enforcement (FACE) program in Boston already foreshadowed this when it found that some longer term residents in Jamaica Plain invested their own "mattress money," personal rainy day savings, as soon as code enforcement dealt with absentee owners (Blaine, 1973). Relatively few bothered to seek federal 3 percent loans. Interviews revealed that before their attitudes toward the neighborhood had become positive, they had felt it a poor investment. When the attitudes did become positive, hidden resources were tapped. The previously mentioned television broadcast simply reinforced these new attitudes like a selective megaphone.

The process that catalyzed attitudes in Jamaica Plain is important to understand because it produced neighborhood confidence. This involves something more than making low interest loans available, since such loans in other sections of the city were perceived as confirmation that conditions were deteriorating.

Neighborhood vitality has just as often been assumed to be a direct function of the age and condition of housing stock. Here too, Boston research refines these assumptions. The potential expansion of Boston's international airport threatened East Boston for years. After organized neighborhood opposition contributed to the redirection of airport expansion, neighborhood investment by existing residents surged ahead. It appears that "weather fronts of low confidence," passing over particular urban neighborhoods, cause low neighborhood investment rather than housing obsolescence or limited resident incomes.

When confidence ebbs, maintainence plummets. When the clouds pass on, revitalization occurs, often without significant population change. Since this frequently happens without public programs and without large scale shifts of population, it must involve changes in perceptions and attitudes that prompt the participants to take a fresh look. The determinants of these ebbs and flows of confidence will become increasingly critical to all who seek to understand and improve the urban predicament.

CONTRASTING ALTERNATIVE RESEARCH APPROACHES

The mainstream of urban research has had a familiar pattern, one that has probably been shaped principally by econometric modeling. Certain assumptions are stated as axiomatic—hypotheses are then derived from these assumptions. For example, housing expenditures on maintenance are assumed to be directly related to available income. The interrelationship among maintenance, fix-up, and property taxation is then hypothesized. Most orthodox urban research consists of seeking data for validation of such propositions in as many situations as possible. Since adequate, clean, hard data for this approach are rarely found, researchers have been unable to detect secondary influences such as owner motivations governing housing expenditures.

The hallmarks of orthodox research are technical proficiency— rigorous emphasis on appropriate sample selection, development of coded survey instruments, factor analyses, and multivariate regressions. Hedonic price indices capture the essence of orthodox research. At this rudimentary stage of theory building these indices are impressive and costly, but inappropriate. An elite urban research fraternity has developed which appears preoccupied with pyrotechnics, seeking that smaller Midwestern city with reliable data that will round out the national sample and which is then surveyed at great taxpayer expense by trained analysts. Meanwhile the alert layman has become aware that housing outlays no longer regularly relate to available income in the assumed way. Why are gays, inter-racial couples, or the Portuguese more likely to be involved in revitalizing a disinvested neighborhood? The orthodox analysts are unable to handle such questions. They defend their approach, saying there are as yet no data clean enough to tease out such subtle differentiations. To them such phenomena are currently below the threshhold of resolution.

A very different style of research is used in other scientific fields to explore puzzling questions. Let us call it enigma-focused research to contrast it with orthodox urban research. Ideally it begins with carefully drawn comparative case studies like Jamaica Plain, from which causality is then inferred. These should be selected to be as alike as possible in most regards, facilitating the detection of salient differences, the enigmas. For example, researchers in one Boston study investigated housing conditions in various neighborhoods made up exclusively of triple-decker structures (BRA/BUO, 1976). Data obtained by household in micro-areas revealed that some elusive factor caused residents in some areas to invest in their homes and caused renters to want to stay, while in comparative areas residents with similar incomes in similar homes sought to move when they could. This led to the discovery of a neighborhood confidence factor (Goetze, 1976).

Enigma-focused research revealed that neighborhood perception and media impact can influence households with rising incomes to stay and invest or to move elsewhere to escape a bad neighborhood image. When reality is obscured, whatever the media reinforce makes the difference. Experimentation through manipulation of media images confirmed not only that these perceptions were important variables, but also that they could be utilized to exert an unexpectedly strong influence on residents' decisions to stay and invest or move. (Rugo, 1979).

Orthodox researchers are unequipped to analyze these dynamics. The orthodox approach requires actual price changes for validation of inferences. Not only are price changes extremely difficult to obtain with adequate rigor, they are also too far behind in time to be useful in detecting such shifts in perception.

Traditional hard data research requires paired sales, knowledge of actual maintenance expenditures, tax payment and abatement histories. It then becomes tangled up in the appropriate discount factor for the local cost of living index while also attempting to correct for changing constant dollar values. Enigma-focused research, on the other hand, simply gathers real estate broker perceptions on changes in market behavior over time, asking, "What strikes you as having changed as you compare these two neighborhoods?" In Boston, it turned out that the time period required to find a buyer for a standard property was a better and simpler indicator of this important "factor x" shaping housing behavior.

In the last eight years a team of researchers in Boston has gained expertise in developing this fresh analytical approach. At first, disparaging remarks like "quick and dirty," or "unsubstantiated evidence," intimidated the researchers and practicing planners. However, orthodox analytical approaches became less and less satisfactory or able to make any substantial contributions.

Meanwhile, the new approaches led to a HUD-funded innovative and successful program of neighborhood confidence building, influencing the public image of marginal neighborhoods (Rugo, 1979) and city-funded direct housing improvement incentives to homeowners (Goetze, 1976). These confirmations of the role neighborhood perception and confidence plays in revitalizing neighborhoods justify unconventional research. Coherence and plausible explanations of causality offer another scientifically acceptable way of confirming hypotheses that orthodox researchers have entirely overlooked.

Konrad Lorenz, the ethologist, emphasized the need for careful description in "The Fashionable Fallacy of Dispensing with Description":

> The current belief that only quantitative procedures are scientific and that the description of structure is superfluous, is a deplorable fallacy, dictated by the "technomorphic" thought-habits acquired by our culture when dealing preponderantly with inorganic matter (Lorenz, 1973: 1–9).

This article should be required reading for all who seek to understand and influence urban systems. The key to the approach lies in detecting changes occuring at the margins and then determining which changes will have the most significant impact. Lorenz, in effect, legitimizes the research approach Boston has instinctively pursued.

Table 4–1 contrasts these alternative research styles while recognizing that each has its place, merits, and drawbacks, and that most actual research lies between these extremes.

FURTHER EXPLORATION OF THE INFLUENCE OF CONTEXT ON NEIGHBORHOOD DYNAMICS

The illustrative case study of Jamaica Plain has shown that household income and dwelling age are not the only significant determinants of housing condition. This section explores other important variables shaping neighborhood dynamics.

While it is easy to discover ways in which cities differ from one another, it is much more important to discover the minimum dimensions that enable meaningful contrasts to be drawn. An eventual research goal would be to develop a taxonomy of cities, and this book should be viewed as a first, tentative step in that direction. Beyond the simplistic Frostbelt/Sunbelt concept, there exists no accepted methodology for contrasting cities. Therefore this discussion will be brief and hypothetical. It is only intended to open up new avenues of research.

At least four dimensions are needed to capture the context of local neighborhood dynamics: metropolitan dynamics, salient central

Table 4—1. **Contrasting Alternative Research Approaches**

Orthodox Research	*Enigma-focused Research*
Assumptions accepted as axiomatic	Assumptions challenged and stereotypes overturned
Oriented toward hypothesis testing and validation	Oriented toward hypothesis generation and detection of fresh enigmas
Survey approach	Case study approach
Focused on the center	Focused on the margins
Broadest possible range for representativeness	Near twin cases sought to enable detection of salient differences
Hard data and rigor-oriented, requiring "clean" data for electronic processing	Seeking salient data, often de nova, interested in explanatory anecdotes, ethnic jokes
End goal: validation	End goal: coherence and insight
Tends to require direct information carefully obtained in methodical surveys	Can utilize indirect information, tease out sub-conscious impressions, draw broader inferences
Practitioners: mandarin priesthood, Ph.Ds and federally sponsored contractors	Practioners: Konrad Lorenz, Jane Jacobs, Eric Hoffer, unconventional outsiders
"Fundable research"	"Quick and dirty"
Unwieldy, difficult to redirect, and expensive	Tactical, versatile, and inexpensive
"Knows more and more about less and less"	Because it is unorthodox, many question its validity

city differentials, citizens' expectations of government, and local administrative context. A discussion of each of these dimensions follows, accompanied by some illustrative inferences. How specific cities contrast in these key dimensions should be made a research focus.

These insights are emerging under a HUD-funded study of neighborhood resource allocation practices in the twenty-eight largest U.S. cities and eight urban counties that Boston began under the direction of the Urban Consortium in 1978.

Metropolitan Dynamic Context:
Dimension One

A better understanding of the national shifts among "go-getters" and "empty-nesters" will improve on the Frostbelt/Sunbelt dichotomy. A rapidly growing metropolis obviously differs from a mature or declining one in many ways. Among the most critical differences are the relative size of various age and class cohorts and local morale which seems associated with growth and decline in a self-fulfilling way. Since people are not equally likely to move at all ages, the net result in growing metropolitan areas, regions with a strong employment base and rich in amenities, is a disproportionately large share of twenty to thirty-nine year olds. This leaves a corresponding deficit wherever they left.

The actual numbers also mask a hidden productivity multiplier because the twenty and thirty year olds, whether laborers or lawyers, tend to work for less compensation than those past middle age.

"Empty-nesters" and retirees are also becoming increasingly mobile. The more affluent and adventurous tend to move farther to more benign climates, bringing their assets and civic influences with them. Declining areas thus develop a second deficit in these older households, further reducing the mature skills, time, and effort normally available and devoted to local affairs. Here again, the impact is greater than the actual numbers. Local unemployment and significant city/suburb splits, while important, are secondary to these overall shifts.

The media seem to amplify these effects. The "dynamics of decline" and their counterpart "the boom of growth" are visibly debated, discussing whether growth is deep and lasting as in Houston or Phoenix, or tied to one industry with ups and downs such as Boeing in Seattle or automobiles in Detroit. This not only further influences where the mobile age groups settle down, but feeds back into the local behavior and expectations of the much larger number of rooted residents. The morale of whole cities has now become an important factor. Just as in neighborhoods, the media exaggerate and reinforce the actual statistical differences. The despondence of Cleveland or Newark, the coping of Baltimore or Boston, and the "can do" of Dallas, Houston, and Southern California already begin to be explained at this macro level.

The fact that transferees from Ohio to Southern California find that equivalent housing will cost them three times what they were previously paying per month suggests how large these differences have recently become. Such divergence in value may also limit these migratory trends.

Salient Central City Differentials: Dimension Two

This category is a necessary catch-all for significant idiosyncratic factors. If it ends up with too much that is unique to specific cities, the usefulness of this taxonomy erodes. Ultimately the value of this dimension lies in discovering important commonalities like regional factors or the role played by different types of geography or transportation networks.

A good beginning lies in pursuing the idea that North America is in fact nine nations, each with its own capital, secondary cities, special problems, and opportunities (Garreau, 1979). (See Table 4—2).

The illegal Chicano aliens without voting rights in Los Angeles, the elderly retirees present only eight months of the year in Phoenix, the Cuban expatriates in Miami, the black majority in Washington, D.C., the gays in San Francisco, the disproportionate number of young singles in Seattle, the large military presence outside San Diego or San Antonio—these are all likely determinants of how a particular city will rate on dimensions three and four.

Local geography and transportation also play an important role. In some cities, situated on the uniform flat plane that preoccupies theoretical modelers and with completed freeway systems, ethnic groups and classes have largely separated out, birds of a feather flocking together. Cleveland exemplifies this. Here the upper class is totally suburban and split from the urban lower class. Further-

Table 4—2.   The Nine Nations of North America

Nation	Capital	Other Major Cities
Ecotopia	San Francisco	Seattle
The Breadbasket	Kansas City	Minneapolis, Winnipeg
The Foundry	Detroit	Cleveland, Pittsburgh, Toronto
New England	Boston	Providence, Hartford, Halifax
Dixie	Atlanta	New Orleans, Birmingham
Mexamerica	Los Angeles	Phoenix, Houston, Monterrey
The Empty Quarter	Denver	Salt Lake City, Calgary, Las Vegas
The Islands	Miami	Havana, San Juan
Quebec	Quebec	Montreal

Source: Developed from Garreau (1979).

more, lower class whites are to the west of the central business district while minorities are to the east. In spite of a population of over two million there is no reason to live close in because one can always drive home in twenty minutes.

On the other hand, in cities with a discontinuous and more interesting topography—steep hillsides, bays, islands, and special views or exposures—as well as those with large bodies of water or incomplete freeway systems, this separating out of the population is constrained. In Seattle, choice urban locations reduced the exodus to the suburbs. In San Francisco and Boston, with a rapid transit alternative and incomplete freeway networks, urban location was further enhanced so neighborhood revitalization commenced sooner. There are more rubbing of shoulders and chance contact between classes and ethnic groups in these constrained growth cities. Additional research should explore whether or not this leads to greater appreciation of diversity and ethnic contrasts, or results in broader input into local government.

Before proceeding to the remaining dimensions that affect neighborhood dynamics, it is important to realize how they might possibly interlink. Figure 4–1 lays them out, from macro to micro. Many already lend themselves to scaling on a continuum. Others will be grouped into types as urban systems become better understood. The links between dimensions can be a valuable research focus. When such differentiations are more rigorously developed, they promise to contribute to better understanding of the determinants of neighborhood dynamics. The dimensions have been arrayed so that they go together, that is, a young, growing metropolis would tend to fall toward the left in each of the dimensions in Figure 4–1, while a mature, declining city will usually fall toward the right. While this may not always be true, deviations become more meaningful when seen in this light. This serves as a kind of null hypothesis.

Citizens' Expectations of Government: Dimension Three

There are sharp differences from city to city in the roles residents currently expect their local government to play. At the same time there is little local awareness that expectations differ widely, even in cities near one another such as Cleveland and Columbus, Ohio. This may be because no measures of expectations exist. The narrow view of the role of the public sector—limiting it to providing sewers, water, roads, schools, and libraries—is one extreme that is generally associated with growth. Arizona exemplifies this through the role of the public sector in Phoenix and surrounding Maricopa County. At

Figure 4–1.   Contextual Dimensions Influencing Neighborhood Trends

1. *Metropolitan Dynamic Context*

Rapidly Growing:
young, energetic
population

High morale: can do

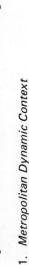

Shrinking:
residual, elderly, and
disadvantaged population

Low morale: need help

2. *Salient Central City Differentials*

● Race and class anomalies
● Sorted out or integrated
● Smooth plain or variated topography
● Completed or fragmented interstate highway system
● Other important anomalies like trauma in recent history

3. *Citizens' Expectations of Government*

A limited bundle

An ever-expanding bundle

Only sewers, roads, water
schools and libraries

Greater benefits:
generous welfare, decent housing
@ 25 percent of income, cradle-to-grave
Medicare, continuing education

Accountability
"I earned it!
I deserve it"

Inured to buck-passing
"I need it, therefore
I have a prior right!"

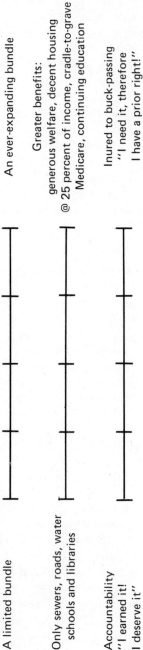

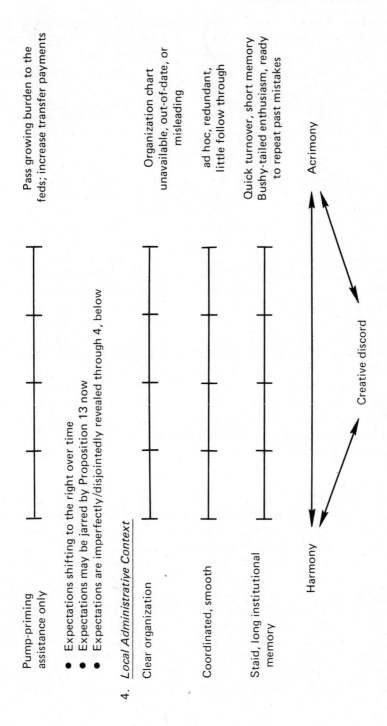

Pump-priming assistance only |————————| Pass growing burden to the feds; increase transfer payments

- Expectations shifting to the right over time
- Expectations may be jarred by Proposition 13 now
- Expectations are imperfectly/disjointedly revealed through 4, below

4. *Local Administrative Context*

Clear organization |————————| Organization chart unavailable, out-of-date, or misleading

Coordinated, smooth |————————| ad hoc, redundant, little follow through

Staid, long institutional memory |————————| Quick turnover, short memory Bushy-tailed enthusiasm, ready to repeat past mistakes

Harmony ⟷ Creative discord ⟷ Acrimony

the other extreme, often associated with decline, lies "the welfare state" with cradle-to-grave health care, public university education, and rhetorically promised high standard decent housing at 25 percent of income for all. On this contextual dimension New York City is far to the right. In fact, most of the Northeast, leading the country in greater welfare benefits, seems "progressive" in demanding more benefits from the public sector. Many expect that Houston and Dallas will eventually increase their public sector role as well, but currently they still fall to the left in Figure 4–1.

In cities on the left column, citizens demand more accountability of their public servants, while those on the right seem to have become more inured to buck-passing. While the difference is clear upon visiting the city hall in any city, the causes are more obscure. Additional research should investigate how much of this difference is due to the local culture and how much is a response to growing bureaucratic complexity.

Two subordinate aspects of citizen expectations deserve special attention. "I earned it, I deserve it" is a dominant and long-standing American ethic that accompanied hard-working immigrants to America. It is placed to the left to contrast with "I need it (or I was here first), therefore I have a prior right," a conflicting ethic expounded by the federal government at least since Lyndon Johnson launched the War on Poverty. The gentrification/displacement, and the red-lining/reinvestment issues are all variants on earn/deserve clashing with needs/rights.

Often paralleling earn/deserve (on the left) is the public's expectation that outside assistance merely serve as pump-primer. Similarly needs/rights corresponds with expectations that the federal government should underwrite everything people think they have a right to expect, but local municipalities lack the tax base to supply. The Arizona–New York City polarity holds true for both of these aspects.

Local performance is judged against local expectations, rendering absolute levels of performance relatively unimportant. For example, Boston residents tend to demand more and better municipal services than Detroit residents. Boston residents expect all streets to be plowed right after a snowstorm and usually gripe about city performance, while in Detroit only arterial plowing is expected and residents willingly pitch in to make the local situation manageable.

Expectations of government have tended to increase over time, shifting each city to the right, although Proposition 13 casts doubt as to whether any continuing shift to the right will be probable. Also, local constituencies themselves change as newcomers with different ethics replace others who move out or die. However, there is no simple, clear indicator of what the citizens expect at any one time from their government. The electoral process only reveals it imperfectly and disjointedly through dimension four.

The gap between expectations and reality will become more critical in the coming period of scarce resources. Tempering expectations may soon be a more effective city endeavor than pursuing unattainable resources.

Local Administrative Context:
Dimension Four

It is important to differentiate three overlapping aspects of local administration. First, it is naive to expect all municipalities to have clear organization charts, or for each bureaucrat loyally to play his or her part in serving the public. Only a few cities like Baltimore, Memphis, or Pittsburgh even approach it. In other cities the organization chart is unavailable, out-of-date, or misleading and new agencies have been created to cover others that function poorly, to play mandated federal roles, to respond on an ad hoc basis to critical issues, or to provide simple patronage.

A second aspect of the local administrative context regards institutional memory and staff turnover. On the left belong jurisdictions where memory seems long, turnover low, and promotions predictable, suggesting that the various municipal actors competently and comfortably fit their roles. On the right belong rapidly changing administrations with much staff turnover, allowing quick exploitation of fresh opportunities but also creating the danger of repeating past mistakes.

The third aspect may be especially useful—while there is harmony to the far left and acrimony to the far right, creative discord, which seems so valuable, fits less neatly onto this continuum. To some degree creative discord, competition, and dissonance, as manifested in San Francisco and Boston, appear to quicken a city's response to changed circumstances. But no one has been able to identify the optimal level, or what generates and maintains it.

Cities such as San Jose, which seem to belong consistently to the left in Figure 4–1, teach us comparatively little. Cleveland, far to the right on all aspects, is now so submerged in acrimony that it seems rational decisionmaking has become suspended. It is difficult to learn much here either. The cities that do not consistently fit to the left or to the right are likely to teach us more. For example, Pittsburgh or Baltimore belong to the right until one reaches the local administrative context, at which point well-coordinated government stands out. Did Pittsburgh's crisis of nearly choking on its own smoke, coupled with large population losses, force a fundamental reappraisal? It is said Baltimore pulled itself together to avoid becoming another Newark.

These dynamics are endlessly fascinating as the press casts the news in terms of personalities. Lindsey of New York, Daley of Chicago, Alioto of San Francisco, were each portrayed as shaping events when they may have actually been little more than an expression of their time and context. Local leadership is deliberately not made a salient dimension because no local individual appears to make such a significant difference.

Applying these dimensions to two illustrative examples suggests how they can increase the understanding of neighborhood context. Contrast the Los Angeles basin with greater New York City. In dimension one, Southern California is growing strongly, absorbing skills and talents, while New York is left with a disproportionately needy population.

In dimension two, the Chicano aliens are a significant factor in Southern California. They work but do not qualify for the fringe benefits of citizenship—unemployment insurance and social security—because their presence is illegal. New Yorkers would hasten to point out that their city is unique and cannot be compared, but there most immigrants, such as Puerto Ricans, are qualified for all benefits.

Along dimensions three and four, in Southern California earn/deserve emerges as dominant, with public resources directed toward organized neighborhoods by authorities that seem as reasonably coordinated as can be expected among multiple jurisdictions. New York City, in contrast, is focused on needs/rights with a discouraging history of attempts to rebuild Bedford-Stuyvesant, and now the South Bronx, while the red tape of Gotham has been proverbial since the days of Tammany Hall.

Most cities that are in decline also have a reduced tax base due to population and resource shifts, rendering them more dependent on federal assistance to provide services that the public expects (dimension three). This federal assistance appears free, but actually comes with detailed administrative regulations and even its own invisible counterpart bureaucracies to oversee that federal goals are met (Yin, 1978). As overall interrelationships between means and ends become obscured by layers of bureaucracy and competing self-interests, confusion results from unrecognized goal conflicts.

The influences of these key dimensions on neighborhood dynamics can already be glimpsed, but more research is needed to confirm them. In Figure 3–3 one might expect a rapidly growing city to have consistently strong neighborhoods, and a declining city with a weak

housing demand to have predominantly weak neighborhoods. However, as complexity increases, resident decisions to stay and maintain or to move and improve come under intangible influences that
media images can manipulate. As a result there can be much more
disinvestment or speculation than logic suggests. Here planners must
discover the intangible forces shaping neighborhood dynamics and
how to influence them.

When planners lose their bearings, as can easily occur in the right-
hand cities if there is no investment in basic research, they seem to
slip from managing change to masking it, attempting to preserve the
status quo or to prove that something can be done, even as the
corollaries of complexity make it less and less possible.

Planners in declining cities drawing upon federal assistance appear
to be straddling a dilemma today—whether to continue increasingly
uncertain efforts to bring back declining neighborhoods, attempting
to house a token few of the disadvantages with special loan funds
and other promising and innovative devices, or to join with the private efforts of college educated, middle class pioneers, people with
whom they easily identify, in the urban revitalization process. There
is a favorable momentum building here and by participating, planners
can appear as masters of a welcome dynamic. If they could square
it with themselves most would choose the latter course, but in doing
so they become distracted from the basic issue: how to help the disadvantaged while maintaining urban homeostasis.

 *Chapter 5*

Deriving A Housing Policy Law

This essay explores the impact of severely fluctuating neighborhood dynamics upon specific properties, revealing how arson and condominium conversions can occur among formerly well-maintained investor-owned multifamily apartments. Since investors and their managers keep good records, neighborhood change can be more easily followed in multifamily properties, but the inferences apply to single family housing as well. The presence of particular owner types not only indicates the current neighborhood dynamic, the market behavior of the owners reveals a new Housing Policy Law: The public welfare is best served when housing benefits and costs for all interests are maintained in a predictable relationship over the long term. Increasing complexity obscures housing values in many urban markets and undermines general welfare. Public interventions that fail to consider the dynamics or violate the Housing Policy Law exacerbate the situation.

TWO CONTRASTING BUILDING CASE HISTORIES

The Boston Redevelopment Authority has compiled detailed histories of representative multifamily buildings in various neighborhoods. The most extreme variations have occurred in the Fenway neighborhood. Here, within walking distance of Symphony Hall, Northeastern University, and the Boston Museum of Fine Arts, a neighborhood called Seven Streets has experienced traumatic changes in the last fifteen years as students displaced long-term family and

elderly tenants, only to find that minorities, then hookers and ad-
dicts, were moving in on their heels. Sensationalizing reporters called
it a disaster, similar to the South Bronx.

Actual data were obtained from over forty multifamily properties
in the immediate area (Goetze, 1977). Since no two buildings are
ever identical, the many actual experiences have been presented as
two sample alternatives related to a prototypical ten-unit property.
The first alternative reflects the experience of buildings in the area
that remained in single, long-term ownership; the second shows the
impact, on the same buildings, of ownership turnover, taking advantage of appreciation, and avoiding losses.

Data were compiled from the records of the Boston Tax Assessor
and Collector-Treasurer, Rent Control Administration, Registry of
Deeds, the Housing Court, and interviews with owners, tenants, managers, investors, lenders, appraisers, and some newspaper reporters.

The Experience with a Single Owner

Table 5—1 reveals the change over the last dozen years in a prototypical ten-unit apartment structure. It shows gross rent, operating
expenses, and property taxes in 1964 and 1976 as well as some financial indicators used in conventional analysis. Because the analysis
leads to significant insights, it is worth following closely.

Annual gross rent (line 1) reflects a change in monthly rents from
around $83 monthly per apartment in 1964 to $200 in 1976, roughly
in step with inflation over the period. Operating expenses (line 2)
more than doubled, while city taxes on the property (line 3) more
than tripled (Boston's unusual tax structure seeks one-third of gross
rents!). The owner's net income before financing (line 4) increased

Table 5—1. One Owner Fenway Building Financial History *(10 Apartments)*

	1964	1976
1. Annual Gross Rent	$10,000	$24,000
2. Operating Expenses	3,300	8,300
3. Property Taxes	2,300	8,000
4. Owner's Net Income (before financing)	4,400	7,700
5. Cap Factor	.088	.128
6. Imputed Market Value	50,000	60,000
7. Outstanding Mortgages	35,000	20,000
8. Owner's Equity	15,000	40,000
9. Gross Rent Multiplier (GRM)	5.0	2.5

Source: Boston Redevelopment Authority, Research Department.

only 75 percent, not in keeping with inflation, because operating expenses and property taxes have claimed more than their share of the increased rents.

This investment in real property has been yielding its one owner a steady but declining return on equity, as the value of the structure declined when measured in constant dollars. ($60,000 in 1976 has less purchasing power than $50,000 did in 1964). This investment resembles a high yield bond in some ways, but is in fact much riskier.

While the market value of the property has risen only marginally (line 6, based on dividing line 4 by line 5, which represents the market rate capitalization factor), the gross rent multiplier (GRM) has dropped from 5.0 to 2.5 (line 9, obtained by dividing line 6 by line 1). This is ominous. At a GRM of 5.0 an investor sees a long time horizon over which he expects capital improvements to pay back. However, at 2.5 he is discouraged from further investments that do not bring a quick return.

The Experience with Owner Turnover

Table 5-2 indicates what has happened to a comparable property that changed hands or was refinanced to enable profit taking. It contains two basic differences from Table 5-1. Data for intervening years (1968-1972) have been introduced, and the property in 1976 has much higher outstanding mortgate indebtedness, giving the latest owner "negative equity." Initially, gross annual rent (line 1) sharply increased due to the influx of student housing demand, but declined after 1972, due to rent control, a changing population, rent skip outs, and vacancies.

Table 5-2. Several Owner Fenway Building Financial History
(10 Apartments)

	1964	1968	1972	1976
1. Gross Annual Rent	$10,000	$17,000	$25,000	$24,000
2. Operating Expenses	3,300	4,000	6,000	8,300
3. Property Taxes	2,300	2,800	6,600	8,000
4. Owner's Net Income (before financing)	4,400	10,200	12,400	7,700
5. Cap Factor	.088	.10	.11	.128
6. Imputed Market Value	50,000	102,000	113,000	60,000
7. Outstanding Mortgages	35,000	80,000	95,000	85,000
8. Owner's Equity	15,000	22,000	18,000	(25,000)
9. Gross Rent Multiplier (GRM)	5.0	6.0	4.5	2.5

Source: Boston Redevelopment Authority, Research Department.

Operating expenses (line 2), on the other hand, were slow to increase with student demand but post–Vietnam inflation and increased heating costs have recently forced expenses sharply up.

Property taxes (line 3) were rising with the general tax rate, but in 1973 the city assessors used rent control data to revise tax assessments in order to collect 30 percent of gross rent in taxes (sic).

Net income before financing (line 4) first soared as a result of strong demand, then plunged because lags in operating expenses coupled with weakened demand.

Market value rose and fell between 1964 and 1976 (line 6). Translating varying net income through the capitalization factor appropriate to that time and location reveals that property value first doubled and then dropped back to nearly its former level. The owner who refinanced or traded saw his $15,000 equity earn him $52,000 (the increase in market value on line 6) between 1964 and 1968, and a further $11,000 between 1968 and 1972. However, from 1972 to 1976 there was a loss in value of $53,000 (change on line 6). If $63,000 was taken out between 1964 and 1972, $53,000 now must be put back in. Who wants to do that?

The gross rent multiplier (line 9), that conventional rule of thumb for judging value, did not warn of impending reversals, but stayed near 5 through 1972. It was generally accepted that property values were roughly five times annual gross rent—and until recently many Boston real estate participants, including potential buyers, would assume from the financial data that the property was worth well over $100,000. In spite of declining market value, fire insurance remained in effect at this higher value, so that in the event of loss, mortgage holders stood to be reimbursed.

VARIOUS INVESTER–OWNER TYPES
SIGNAL MARKET CHANGES

New breeds of investors thrive in these rapidly shifting markets. If they do not actually cause the shifts, their presence at least indicates them. Table 5–3 caricatures seven discernible prototypes of owners encountered in the BRA study of multifamily investor-owned housing in all parts of Boston. Before examining their succession, a few brief words on the types are in order.

Established Owners and *Blue Collar Investors* (Types A and B) have traditionally and ably served tenant housing needs in stable markets. As Table 5–3 elaborates, they have a long and steady perspective, acting as trustworthy custodians for their part of the housing

Table 5-3.   Various Investor Types Owning Multifamily Housing

Type A   *Established Owners/Managers (Blue-Bloods)*
- Like stable markets
- In business a long time for steady returns
- Integrity, pride in waiting list of tenants
- Objective: steady earnings = f (quality, steady services)
- Careful selection of choice, qualified tenants
- Tend to have relatively low mortgages or own outright

Type B   *Blue-collar Investors*
- Promote stable markets
- In business for their own (or survivors') financial security
- Unsophisticated
- Objective: equity to cover old age
- Minimize mortgages, own outright if possible
- Tend to cluster holdings near their own residence
- Always on hand to do repairs on weekends, evenings
- Easily and unwittingly overwhelmed by changes
- Ill-equipped to deal with complexity of rent control, housing court, tax abatements, etc.

Type C   *Traders*
- Speculate in rising markets
- Seek leverage and rapid appreciation of equity
- Objective: reap gains from appreciation upon resale
- Increase gross rent and capitalize on it by selling at a favorable price
- Tenants incidental; there only to keep building occupied and to demonstrate rent potential to next investor
- Minimize personal exposure (put in little time or money to maintain property)
- Concentrate on cosmetics that would increase resale price
- Polarized tenant-landlord relationships likely

Type D   *Operators*
- Derive profits from operations in weak market areas where no one else will supply housing—the low-end of the housing spectrum
- Stereotyped as the slumlord, around since at least 1960s
- Can't be dislodged because of problem of relocating tenants
- Objective: high annual returns (attendant high risks)
- Will pay taxes only as advantageous but counting on "end game" (4-5 years before City forecloses)
- Accept and pocket whatever they can of rents obtained
- Minimize taxes and maintenance outlays
- Acquire without conventional mortgage, perhaps take over existing mortgage or obtain mortgage from seller
- Properties may be encumbered with second mortgages, liens, etc.
- Virtually no tenant selection exercised, more likely than most to take welfare referrals to avoid vacancies
- Often own "worst" housing in neighborhood, causing abutters to despise them, seek their removal
- Tenant-landlord polarization
- Likely to be in or get into tax delinquency

(Table 5-3. continued overleaf)

Table 5–3. continued

Type E   *Shareholders*

- Attracted to housing as investment opportunity
- Professionals pool money to invest; form limited partnerships
- Buy at "favorable GRM's" and hope to make money through tax advantages—shelters, artificial losses
- Have limited grasp of housing issues, and responsibilities, (other than economic), but may retain a competent management team which is a critical element in delivery of decent housing services

Type F   *Rehabbers and Developers*

- Work in recycling neighborhoods and renewal areas
- Often flourished under federal assistance and now have enormous appetite for more subsidies, and/or tax breaks
- Adept at complex problems, handling red tape
- Politically shrewd, often manipulative to the extent of shaping administration of regulatory agencies
- Make their money at front end, ownership incidental
- Shapers of new market trends
- Likely to derive special advantages from tax collection and rent control system
- Increasingly the envy or model of other entrepreneurs

Type G   *Special Forces* (Distressed Property Handlers)

- Specialize in newest gimicks, take over where others leave off
- Always one step ahead of any regulatory agency (municipal, government, IRS, etc.)
- Profits are losses and losses are very profitable
- Calibre of management team, if such exists at all, depends on owner's view of what will return greatest profit within his limited time frame

---

Source: Goetze (1978).

inventory. While they easily ride out the ebbs and flows of the market as long-term owners, they have a low tolerance for administrative complexity.

Traders (Type C) speculate in rising markets and never intend to own or manage their properties for long. Ideally they just take options, but in fact they outbid types A and B in rising markets, taking over.

Operators (Type D) come closest to the stereotypical slumlord and signal a weak or declining housing market. While deterioration proceeds with both traders and operators, each indicates opposite market tendencies and must not be confused with the other. The operators become or remain owners of properties no one else wants or can handle. They milk the cash flow, and cut all the corners they can. While traders speculate in anticipated value, operators manage what has indeterminate value.

Shareholders (Type E) dream they can be Zeckendorfs or pursue business school fantasies, but have limited grasp of the actual complexities of housing investment. Therefore, traders who anticipate a deterioration in market climate frequently manage to sell to shareholders.

Rehabbers and *Developers* (Type F) have come into existence in response to the complex public housing assistance programs and are now the ones most able to make these programs deliver. As an interest group they interact closely (some say manipulate) public administrators and policymakers at the city, state, and national level.

Special Forces (Type G) are so unconventional that they defy categorization, but their wide-ranging abilities impress all with whom they interact. Some were formerly traders and now handle conversions to condominiums and the like. Rehabbers may be another simple subset of this type.

Reality is seldom as pure as this typology suggests, but once the prototypes are clear and one knows what to look for, differentiating actual investors is relatively simple. Then, like meteorologists, one can track the behavior of these various investor types to identify shifts in market climate.

Established owners and blue collar investors are in business to deliver housing services, not to profit at the margin. The financial picture sketched in Table 5—1 suggests how such owners are faring in the Fenway area. They can survive as long as they do not lose the old 6 percent mortgage, but in the current uncertain and fluctuating market climate they are rarely replaced by their own type. The type of owners replacing others at turnover signals prevailing market perception. In Table 5—2, traders predominated among buyers during the 1960s. However, by 1972, turnover brought in shareholders lured by the astounding appreciation and returns on equity that traders were able to show. By 1976 operators, distressed property handlers, and even a few rehabbers were in evidence. Traders attracted by the spectacular gains through 1964 knew enough to sell out by 1972. Often those buying at this point were first-time investors who, while astute enough on the paper benefits of ownership, understood few of the complexities involved in property management. The shareholders who bought after 1970 with highly leveraged and costly financing found themselves in trouble if they paid all expenses, taxes, and debt service. They either evolved into operators, rehabbers, or distressed property handlers or transferred their properties to these types.

In the past, such owners would have been left to suffer the consequences of their bad judgment, but in the Seven Streets area, things took a more sinister turn: arson. Fire insurance policies written at the time of highest value covered more than market value. In many instances, traders arranged or provided mortgages, which by law have prior claim on insurance compensation in case of fire destroying the property.

The properties under study in the Fenway area have in fact experienced numerous fires of suspicious origin, prompting investigations. In October 1977 an arson ring was exposed, indicting several with dealings in the Fenway. While some fires appeared to be the result of tenant negligence, many others seemed to have been set. Aging mechanical systems and deferred maintenance also played a role. To confuse matters even more, some said tenants might also have had motives for arson, since burn-out victims get priority for public assistance and relocation. Media stories compounded the confusion, destroyed any residual market confidence in the area, and failed to illuminate any of the underlying causes.

Recently rehabbers have appeared, taking options on properties in the area because past public policy has given priority in allocating scarce federal assistance to such distressed urban sections. Rehabbers anticipate the media and public clamor to revitalize the Seven Streets area and are preparing for the expected commitment of Section 8 rental assistance to redevelopers.

The Seven Streets area also offers a significant counterpoint. In some nearby properties still in long-term Type A ownership, rents remained modest, housing conditions good, and tenants satisfied. These were often cited as proof that decent owners could survive with the city's rent control and tax policies. However, research revealed that they stopped paying taxes several years ago. One owner reasoned: "I don't like rent control; if I don't pay my taxes I won't need to increase rent; I will thereby avoid tenant polarization and turnover; and finally when the inevitable reckoning hits the other properties, mine will survive." Such shrewdness has paid off so far, and Boston's Collector-Treasurer finds it difficult to deal harshly with this successful owner to collect back taxes when the city is razing nearby arson-damaged properties (also in tax delinquency) at public expense.

The local market is developing an unexpected solution to this dilemma. Young, more affluent households in higher income tax brackets are now buying condominiums nearby. Buildings that have been well maintained by long-term owners are excellent prospects for conversion. Properties currently renting for $240 per month are worth less than $6000 per unit. However, with a little fix-up they become easily worth $30,000 per unit as condominiums today, five times as much! As the area acquires a little class, these values rise to $50,000, promising an excellent return to those households able to put down $6000 as equity. In fact, the carrying costs for a childless two-income household earning $40,000, after taking the mortgage interest and property tax deductions against federal income taxes, are little higher than the former rents. This has already begun in the Seven Streets area. Table 5—4 completes the two alternatives for the hypothetical ten-unit property.

The single owner building is shown as having been converted to condominiums in 1980. In hindsight there was no other way out unless the city was prepared to forgive past taxes and abate current levies. The property then houses a much higher income class and everyone, except the original tenants, has benefitted. Tax arrears were paid off, fix-up occurred, current local tax yield nearly doubled, the lenders converted an uncertain low interest $10,000 mortgage that was little more than an annoyance into $240,000 in secure mortgages to resident owners at 11 percent interest. The only bitter note in this happy ending would be if the conversion happened so swiftly that the prior tenants felt displaced.

The several owner building had provided some windfall gains in its time, but the losses were passed on through suspicious fires to all insurance policy holders. The building of course is no longer there, so it neither shelters needy people nor blights the prospects of revitalization spurred by the young sophisticates nearby.

A NOTE ABOUT ARSON

Arson is a hidden crime that is beginning to thrive on complexity (Massachusetts Arson Task Force, 1979). Although there are no reliable statistics on arson, its economic costs are passed on through higher insurance premiums while the current arrest and conviction rates are extremely low.

Two primary dynamics produce arson. It occurs where the gains (financial or psychological) far exceed the risks of detection and punishment, and where the self-interests of the individuals whose actions could discourage arson no longer discourage it. Arson-for-profit is likely to increase in destabilized urban areas because over-insurance is now encouraged by available Fair Access to Insurance Requirements (FAIR) Plan insurance. This higher insurance coverage both yields brokers higher commissions and pays the insurers the resources they need to offset losses—a vicious circle. The insured properties

Table 5–4. Comparative Financial Histories

ONE OWNER Fenway Building Terminates in Conversion to Condominiums

	1964	1968	1972	1976	1980	CONDO
1. Gross Annual Rent	$10,000			$24,000	$28,800	$38,300 [1]
2. Operating Expenses	3,300			8,300	10,100	10,000
3. Property Taxes	2,300			8,000	10,000	19,000 [2]
4. Owner's Net Income (before financing)	4,400			7,700	8,700	
5. Cap Factor	.088			.128	.15	
6. Imputed Market Value	50,000			60,000	58,000	300,000
7. Outstanding Mortgages	35,000			20,000	10,000	240,000 [3]
8. Owner's Equity	15,000			40,000	48,000	60,000
9. Gross Rent Multiplier (GRM)	5.0			2.5	1.7	

Source: See Table 5–1.

Table 5-4. continued

SEVERAL OWNER Fenway Building Terminates in Arson

	1964	1968	1972	1976	1980
1. Gross Annual Rent	$10,000	$17,000	$75,000	$24,000	A
2. Operating Expenses	3,300	4,000	6,000	8,300	R
3. Property Taxes	2,300	2,800	6,600	8,000	S
					O
4. Owner's Net Income (before financing)	4,400	10,200	12,400	7,700	N
5. Cap Factor	.088	.10	.11	.128	
6. Imputed Market Value	50,000	102,000	113,000	60,000	100,000[4]
7. Outstanding Mortgages	35,000	80,000	95,000	85,000	
8. Owner's Equity	15,000	22,000	18,000	(25,000)	
9. Gross Rent Multiplier (GRM)	5.0	6.0	4.5	2.5	

Source: See Table 5-2.

1. Annual outlays for the 10 condominiums, *including* financing.
2. Property reassessed, based on new use.
3. Ten separate owner mortgages.
4. Insurance settlement after total damage by fire.

are frequently declining in value and tangled in title, making arrest and prosecution difficult even when authorities have reason for suspicion. Such insurance has already become a convenient form of federally underwritten business risk insurance for creditors with a bad loan.

The prevalence of arson could increase dramatically as urban property values become less and less certain, as responsibilities are diffused among more and more roles in the system, and as the overall sense of community erodes, abdicating responsibility for the disadvantaged to the government. Special programs focusing on detection and prosecution of arson will prove futile if urban complexity and uncertainty are not addressed at the same time.

PUBLIC POLICY INFERENCES

These scenarios of change ending in arson and conversion to condominiums must be troubling to policymakers unequipped to deal with the new realities. This was never a case of normal filtration. Maintaining the stock so that decent rental housing continues indefinitely is a valid housing goal, but not easy to attain through means currently within the policymaker's grasp.

It is useful to review what went wrong. Problems began when the relationship between income and expenses became unpredictable. When income outstrips expenses speculation results, drawing in the less beneficial owners, the traders and shareholders. On the other hand, when expenses climb faster than income, other suboptimal ownership styles arise, like operators, distressed property handlers, and rehabbers. In the long run, even responsible interests bow to economic realities and sell to interests that can profit, whether arsonists or young condominium buyers. To attempt to control rents or prevent condominium conversion simply postpones the reckoning.

Table 5—4 reveals that excess demand started the deterioration cycle in 1964 by raising income while expenses and taxes remained low, which suddenly increased the value. Public policy should have immediately either controlled the rents or taxed away the excess profits. Since the city did not do this, traders entered. The "tax brake" applied by the normal order of events between 1968 and 1972 appears about right, but when compounded between 1972 and 1976 by rising heating costs, myopic rent controls applied too late, more taxes, and a less stable tenantry, some housing is irrevocably on the way to destruction. The root of the problem is lack of an adequate public policy. Considering all the properties which had windfall gains taken out, arsonists wrote the final chapter for some, while

Section 8 is belatedly used in attempts to maintain the rest. It is likely to fail.

Various owner types only signal the particular market climate, responding to factors like the advent of students. Acting alone, they cannot actually cause market change. However, their actions frequently exacerbate the market and for this reason they are often assumed to be the cause.

The policy challenge is to identify stabilizing actions that can overcome the destabilizing activities of the various owner types. Once the underlying forces are understood, the remedies become clearer. The solution lies in obeying a deceptively simple but far-reaching Housing Policy Law: *The public welfare is best served when housing income and expenses are maintained in a predictable relationship.* Any measure that increases complexity and reduces predictability must first demonstrate to all interests that benefits outweigh the potential drawbacks. All the familiar policy tools may be suitable: rent control and subsidies on the income side; and measures such as taxes and code enforcement on the expense side. The challenge lies in knowing how and when to apply them, and very little is known about this as yet.

Past housing failures or counterintuitive results can be explained as a result of applying the familiar tools in ways that oppose this fundamental law. In a stable market, income and expenses are maintained in a predictable relationship. Local checks and balances, homeostatic forces acting on the neighborhood housing system, generally seem to have maintained this stability in the past. If one regards stability as the Golden Mean, then one must recognize that housing markets can on the one side veer into disinvestment, and on the other, veer into speculation. Table 5−5 lays out some of the associated pathologies and their remedies.

The Housing Policy Law requires steering a middle course between speculation and disinvestment—between excess demand and excess supply. Speculators and slumlords were thought to refer to the same pathology: greed in housing suppliers. However, one must now differentiate between them, dividing them into traders and operators.

To bring income into line with expenses, policymakers can influence rents, taxes, code enforcement standards, or neighborhood image, *but they must do it in ways that appear fair and predictable to all participants in the system*, not just immediate beneficiaries. If subsidies are applied, they must equitably go to all qualified recipients. To subsidize the rents of only a few owners in a declining market may introduce destabilizing inequities from the point of view of abutting owners, or even raise the operating expenses of all owners,

Table 5–5. Policy Mean Lies Between Extremes

	Extreme (+) *Imbalance*	*Stable* *Balance*	*Extreme (−)* *Imbalance*
Symptoms (Causes?)	Rising market Speculation Excess demand Raving press	G O L D E	Declining market Disinvestment Excess supply Bad press
Indicators	Traders Income > expenses	N	Operators Income < expenses
Corrective Remedies	Decrease income Raise expenses Control rents Raise taxes Enforce code	M E A N	Subsidize rent w/o stigma Abate taxes Boost neighborhood image

Source: Goetze (1978).

depending on how the local system responds to the intervention. This only further destabilizes the neighborhood market. A successful policy approach must consider and anticipate the reactions of all affected interests before intervening. Inequity or unpredictability, even if unintentional, is worse than doing nothing. Benign neglect at least allows homeostatic forces to fight market imbalances, whereas blind interventions frequently override the natural stabilizing mechanisms.

Chapter 6

Further Exploration of
Neighborhood Dynamics

The previous chapter derived a housing policy law from economic data on multifamily properties where explicit financial considerations govern behavior. This chapter examines the changing dynamics in homeownership neighborhoods where social forces and psychology play a much greater role. Predictability, fairness, and sense of control of the neighborhood situation influence behavior here as well. Specific buyer motivations can again serve to indicate changing dynamics to policymakers.

Homeostasis, internal forces exerting checks and balances on behavior affecting the community, was the most effective defense for handling threats to neighborhood viability in the past. However, many changes in society now threaten to upset neighborhood stability and confidence. These range from greater mobility and new lifestyles to many more public interventions. Few are aware of how these changes alter local behavior. In this complex network of participants red-lining was self-fulfilling. But now, as some neighborhoods are rediscovered, speculation becomes a problem.

For continued neighborhood viability, outside actions must reinforce beneficial neighborhood norms and not intervene as if they did not exist. Blind intervention, even with good intentions, can only do more harm than good as less sophisticated residents may believe unattainable promises or develop a dependence on assistance that cannot be sustained in the long run.

HOMEOSTASIS

Any neighborhood has a future that is woven from countless individual housing actions: decisions to buy, to maintain, to improve, to enlarge, to invest, to show off, *or not*, depending on how the many participants see such actions rewarding them, improving their comfort, well-being, or status. Most neighborhoods maintain themselves without more regulations telling residents when to paint, how often to cut their lawn, or how to control their children or pets; yet what shapes decent behavior is seldom considered.

Social norms and other neighborhood coping mechanisms invisibly control most behavior and prevent unacceptable actions like parking across another's driveway, driving over a neighbor's lawn, playing loud music late at night, or, in some neighborhoods, letting crabgrass go to seed. Although nearly invisible, these norms shape most behavior. They, not the police, prevent the flip-top cans from being left in the neighbor's lawn. They, not a government program, initiate most spring cleanups. Most infractions are handled among the residents. Kids do not spray paint or break windows in another home unless they feel they can get away with it. Civil forces normally control uncivil actions, and only in exceptional cases are the police called in to a healthy neighborhood. Ordinances like leash laws, curb your dog, or no overnight on-street parking have only recently been developed. Zoning itself is only fifty years old.

Such behavior is strongly bound to culture. Many immigrant groups, despite their poverty, had rigid strictures about appropriate behavior. Many ethnic communities have fewer burglaries and appear safer than the neighborhoods where today's young and affluent are settling down.

Neighborhood change is an ambiguous code phrase often used to signal the belief that the neighborhood coping mechanisms are becoming overloaded and the social norms may break down. Many use the expression "neighborhood change" upon the entry of minorities, but the coming of students, young professionals, communes, or other households of unrelated individuals can similarly interfere with these traditional coping mechanisms. Neighborhood confidence is the conviction on the part of residents and others in touch with the neighborhood that change will not come at a rate or in ways that prevent these social norms from controlling events.

Examples of such convictions abound in all metropolitan areas and at virtually all income levels. Consider that one can visit most neighborhoods and leave one's car parked on the street without worry that it will have been broken into or stolen, stripped, had its tires slashed, or been spray-painted with grafitti like a New York subway car. However, if dented by someone else, will that person have left a note under the windshield wiper? Actually much more subtle differentiations are continually made by home buyers and prospective tenants, but this illustrates the presence or absence of invisible social norms controlling behavior in these neighborhoods. Since the mechanisms *are* invisible, the owner of a foreign car with radial tires finds it easier to avoid entire neighborhoods than to take chances testing them as described above. Thereby a kind of psychological red-lining sets in, classifying neighborhoods by simple stereotypes. To some degree everyone does this.

The reader might assume that beneficial social norms are a function of higher social class and that lack of adequate coping mechanisms is associated with poverty, housing projects and the disadvantaged. Rather, they are a function of accountability and knowing when anything is out of place. Property may be least safe where many transients such as students live.

In traditional neighborhoods, strong social norms link residents into cooperative interdependence, thereby maintaining a sense of community but stifling exploratory behavior with silent strictures that say in effect, "Not here you don't." Today this seems needlessly oppressive to many, and the most liberated are creating new environments that then sometimes break down. Tenants and landlords traditionally met each other's needs symbiotically, but now role definitions are in flux. In Cambridge, Massachusetts, for example, some shrewd tenants under rent control are trying both to preserve their low rents and to force regular hot water from unwilling owners through the courts. Just as the traditional marriage ceremony has given way to a written legal Contract of Cohabitation among many there, living in Cambridge is evolving without the traditional understandings between fellow residents that neighborhood coping mechanisms and social norms provide.

When community norms erode, the disadvantaged are the first to be hurt or preyed upon while the more able either remain unaware or take care of themselves. The latter, as they tire of such experimentation, find it easier to move into other neighborhoods where homeostasis is still intact than to reconstruct these elusive norms where they have broken down. This then contributes to housing demand in stable neighborhoods that were recently seen as becoming obsolete.

THE INCREASING ROLE OF STATUS

It is easy to understand moving in order to avoid hassles or in order to be in an area where amenities are already there instead of trying to develop them in existing neighborhoods. However, status seeking is also playing an increasing role in shaping urban neighborhood dynamics. The housing system resembles a gigantic game of musical chairs, but some chairs convey status and special opportunities while others stigmatize their occupants.

The element of status and stigma in housing has become more pronounced with the accelerating mobility since World War II. Increasingly there is crowding and bidding up of prices to get into certain neighborhoods, while other areas are being deserted—as if those once caught in declining areas get counted out of the game.

Beshers (1962) has observed that virtually all American households, regardless of whether they are headed by high school dropouts or by lawyers, instinctively rank each other's standing on a social ladder. Furthermore, each believes it has earned its position on a particular rung, viewing those below as less resourceful, while seeing those above as simply more lucky. As complexity increases so does the belief that luck and poverty might be contagious.

SOME RECENT RESEARCH
ON NEIGHBORHOODS

Static typologies of social neighborhoods can form the basis of a system for detecting neighborhood change, but ready indicators of change are not yet available. The research of the Warrens is a good beginning (Warren, 1978). Here three elements—degree of identity, degree of interaction, and nature of outside linkages—are used to differentiate six neighborhood types. Further investigations examine how each type processes information by differentiating opinion sharing, media absorption, and responsiveness to outside informants.

Figure 6–1 summarizes the Warren typology. To understand neighborhood change this approach needs to be followed up to determine how prevalent each type currently is in various cities, and how each evolves over time.

Clay (1978) has independently surveyed revitalizing neighborhoods. He differentiated neighborhoods undergoing gentrification through newcomers from those being upgraded by incumbents, their long-term residents. Clay focused primarily on planning attributes such as distance from central business district, stock type, and relationship to public programs.

Neither the Warrens' nor Clay's research has reached the point of clear policy applications since they ignore change over time. However, ecological metaphors of invasion and succession can be applied to neighborhoods as new types of residents try out and sometimes take hold or make way for still different types to dominate a neighborhood (Pattison, 1977; Gale, 1977; Anderson, 1977).

Identifying the ways in which newcomers contrast with existing residents will help policymakers understand and monitor the revitalization process. This first requires examining various housing markets.

NEIGHBORHOOD HOUSING MARKETS

When a neighborhood begins to change, there may often no longer be any natural forces to arise and counteract that change. For continued stability it is necessary for every change from an equilibrium to be counteracted by a tendency in the opposite direction.

Increasing instability characterizes many contemporary urban neighborhoods. The reactions that follow change often magnify the effect, resulting in increasingly rapid and dramatic fluctuations. In such flux, the impacts of housing policy interventions have not only become unpredictable, they may be making the situation worse.

Declining Markets

For illustrative purposes, consider a hypothetical neighborhood of resident-owned homes. Assume that fifty structures come up for sale annually because of deaths, job transfers, changes in household size, and so forth. To maintain balance, fifty new homeowners must take their place. The key to neighborhood dynamics lies in understanding this replacement process. A balance between the number of buyers and sellers is not automatic. It is a complex process involving many participants. Each communicates to others in subtle and often counterintuitive ways.

Isolated incidents, such as difficulties in obtaining conventional financing, or homeowners' insurance cancellations, may be interpreted by brokers, residents, and potential buyers in ways that negatively affect replacement housing demand.

If only forty-five qualified buyers appear interested in the neighborhood, the other five structures still go somewhere. They may be sold to absentee owners or to other buyers who are seen as incompatible with neighborhood norms.

There may be instances in which the seller takes back a mortgage (if credit difficulties appear to be a barrier to obtaining enough qualified buyers), or an unsold structure may be rented to just anyone while the owner or estate executors wait. These events may trigger complex chain reactions among many of the other resident households, as well as those with roles in the neighborhood housing market, such as brokers, appraisers, and lenders.

Figure 6–1.   The Warrens' Neighborhood Typology

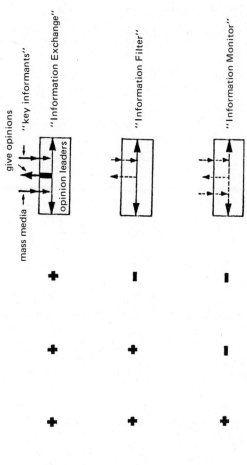

Different Types of Neighborhoods

Type	Identity*	Interaction†	Linkages‡
Integral A cosmopolitan as well as a local center. Individuals are in close contact. They share many concerns. They participate in activities of the larger community.	+	+	+
Parochial A neighborhood having a strong ethnic identity or homogeneous character. Self-contained, independent of larger community. Has ways to screen out what does not conform to its own norms.	+	+	−
Diffuse Often homogeneous setting ranging from a new subdivision to an inner-city housing project. Has many things in common. However, there is no active internal life. Not tied into the larger community. Little local involvement with neighbors.	+	−	−

Neighborhood Information Processing

"Information Exchange"

give opinions → "key informants"

mass media → opinion leaders

"Information Filter"

"Information Monitor"

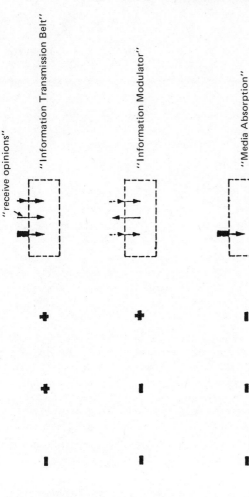

"receive opinions"

"Information Transmission Belt"

"Information Modulator"

"Media Absorption"

Stepping-Stone

An active neighborhood. A game of "musical chairs." People participate in neighborhood activities *not* because they identify with the neighborhood but often to "get ahead" in a career or some other nonlocal point of destination.

Transitory

A neighborhood where population change has been or is occurring. Often breaks up into little clusters of people—frequently "oldtimers" and newcomers are separated. Little collective actions or organization takes place.

Anomic

It's really a nonneighborhood. Highly atomized; no cohesion. Great social distance between people. No protective barriers to outside influences making it responsive to some outside change. It lacks the capacity to mobilize for common actions from within.

*Identity—How much do people feel they belong and share a common destiny, a sense of neighborhood consciousness?

†Interaction—How often and with what number of neighbors do people visit and interact in one year?

‡Linkages—What channels exist between residents and outside groups and those who bring outside news into the neighborhood?

Source: Warrens, *The Neighborhood Organizer's Handbook*, 1977, p. 96, 97, 127.

While all the repercussions cannot be examined here, a number are obvious. Some discretionary sales will result from abutting residents who fear that factors beyond their control will downgrade the neighborhood. Rather than fifty houses seeking replacement buyers in the next year, more than seventy may be on the market, and simultaneously the former reservoir of compatible replacement buyers is likely to diminish. Countless other residents, while not actually deciding to sell, nevertheless adopt more of a wait-and-see attitude regarding home improvements. They wonder whether it makes sense to continue investing in their homes.

Determining reality becomes more problematic than usual. Various housing participants, individually and subjectively, draw their own conclusions about the future of the neighborhood. Stereotyping and prejudice significantly shape many of these individual assumptions, which easily become self-fulfilling convictions. Media coverage of neighborhood events, regardless of their actual importance, is often misinterpreted in wide-ranging ways, reinforcing unspoken negative expectations on the part of a host of differing interests.

The additional housing listings bring more market forces into play. Whereas word-of-mouth may formerly have attracted ample replacement buyers, now brokers, advertising, and for sale signs become increasingly important, raising a new awareness or altering the previous self-perceptions of the community. Remarks of a few disgruntled residents, bad-mouthing the area because of the way they feel, become news that further exacerbates the supply and demand imbalance and inclines insurers and appraisers to be especially conservative in judging future risks. "White flight" illustrates this issue.

The availability of FHA mortgage insurance which enables families with minimal down payments to buy at no risk to the lender (and with no real financial stake themselves), coupled with FAIR plan home fire insurance (which sometimes invites arson), can unintentionally complete the breakdown of the healthy system. When long-term residents experience cancellations of regular home insurance and assignment to the FAIR plan they become aware of change. If the conventional participants with a direct stake in the neighborhood thereupon leave, the area is left to the disadvantaged, who become prey for those who act with impunity.

At this point, change becomes traumatic. Some households are overwhelmed by a fear that in the future the neighborhood will no longer be controlled by its residents.

Impact of FHA-Insured Lending. Once the cycle of decline begins, availability of easier credit can become counterproductive, as revealed by an analysis of the impact of FHA-insured one- to four-family mortgages in Boston.

Data obtained as a result of the Massachusetts Banking Commission's regulations on home mortgage disclosure show how a racially changing neighborhood market can be weakened as a result of self-fulfilling prophecies made by homeowners, potential buyers, brokers, and lenders.

Table 6–1 shows changes in the type of mortgages involved in sales in the eastern portion of Boston's census tract 1404. This neighborhood of nearly 1,000 structures, mainly singles, has a normal annual ownership turnover of 5 percent (1973) and 7 percent (1976). However, the number of low down-payment mortgages has doubled (from 19 to 39) while the number of conventional down-payment mortgages remained virtually the same (26 to 27). The neighborhood had become so aware of the change that 350 residents gathered in a community meeting in August 1976 to hurl allegations of blockbusting at real estate brokers and red-lining at lenders. Yet, to individual lenders or brokers, or even to a statistician looking at the pattern of sales on a map, little change is evident. May 1973 and May 1976 show a similar scattering of sales, and only close inspection shows the increase in low down-payment sales in 1976. Yet the tenor of the community has definitely altered in three years. Without easy credit, the fear of accelerating decline would be less likely to sweep the neighborhood.

Analysis of other Boston neighborhoods suggests that "FHA only" means it is widely believed that only government-insured mortgages are available, suggesting racial change, mortgage foreclosures, and abandoned houses. If many banks insist on government insurance and are unwilling to loan conventionally to buyers who can make down-payments, it would seem a prudent buyer's suspicions are warranted. The stigma discourages some potential buyers with

Table 6–1. Home Mortgages in Census Tract 1404, Boston, Massachusetts

Type of Mortgage	Year	
	1973	*1976*
Conventional down-payment (at least 20 percent equity)	26	27
Low down-payment (FHA–insured)	19	39
Total	45	66

Source: Boston Redevelopment Authority, Research Department.

down-payments, and more are discouraged by the bureaucratic hassles entailed by government insurance.

The headaches of those who sell under FHA—having to pay points on buyers' mortgages, to fix-up even when the buyer wishes to improve the housing his own way, and to face new red tape and delays, makes it clear to residents that things have changed. Bureaucracy intrudes upon and distorts self-interests in shaping the dynamics. Like Gresham's Law, the government-supported programs can drive out conventional buyers, brokers, lenders, and, finally, many of the existing resident owners.

The process selectively winnows out the stronger buyers, weakening the market. Brokers reinforce this selection process by the way they influence housing demand and stress status and security. Whether they do this deliberately or inadvertently, the result is the same: it sharpens the self-fulfilling process of destabilizing, negative feedback.

Rising Markets

Revitalization is a resurgence of confidence in a neighborhood's future, often a reaction signaling that the neighborhood was too pessimistically viewed by the web of participants affecting it. In the most extreme cases, a very visible in-migration of more affluent newcomers signals this change in confidence. It is a process the British call "gentrification," in which higher class residents discover the neighborhood and take it over. One consequence of gentrification may be displacement of existing residents as a result of speculation.

Gentrification. In 1950 an area near Boston's downtown, later called Bay Village, was very shabby and contained many lodging houses with high transiency. It underwent gentrification in four stages (Pattison, 1977). Stage One began as members of the gay community, *risk oblivious* and with few choices open to them, completely renovated some of the most deteriorated properties for themselves and others. Initially there was little displacement and conventional financing was very difficult to obtain. In Stage Two an alert real estate broker who had recently moved in himself began promoting the neighborhood to *risk-and-gain-conscious* young professionals seeking bargains. The area was given the name Bay Village and the Bay Village Neighborhood Association was formed by a core of long-term residents to improve its image and obtain some neighborhood improvements. Market demand increased, leading to the conversion of more rooming houses and some displacement. Financing was still a problem.

In Stage Three, Urban Renewal designation occurred, leading to new sidewalks, lights, and parks, and making financing more widely available. As a result, this revitalized area now draws in middle and upper income families paying top dollar who are *risk-averse.* The resident socio-economic class of the 1940s has been replaced fairly gradually by a higher one.

Since this process now happens more suddenly in many cities, policymakers need indicators of the stages. The household types moving in are the best available indicators; if there is no noteworthy in-migration, there need be no concern about gentrification or displacement.

Newcomers can be ranked along a continuum from pioneers to stragglers:

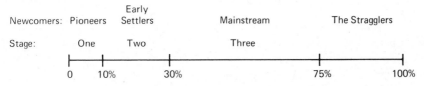

Pioneers, or innovators, are largely self-directed, often seen by others as eccentrics. They try out what appear to be wild (and possibly exciting) places. Some survive in the unlikeliest environments; others are thrown back. But their potential followers, the early settlers, are watching them, interested in how they fare. The pioneer is present in many neighborhoods that never reach Stage Two.

Early settlers, the early adopters and trendsetters for the mainstream, are the leading edge of significant population change. Whereas pioneers may be independent loners, the early settlers are often evangelistic, bargain-oriented, able to check things out on their own, and eager to sell it to others. Being risk and gain conscious, early settlers are less concerned about their relationship with existing residents than whether other settlers are following (to confirm that they have found a bargain). The young sophisticates making the news, rediscovering urban living, are mainly early settlers arranging their own fix-up, hanging plants, and showing their homes.

The *mainstream* are the young, more affluent, two-career households likely to follow the early settlers, developing a new population surge from the stream that formerly only flowed to the suburbs. If there are too many or if they come too fast, they inflate property values. Each member wants to be seen ahead of the trend and invests dearly, confirming the bargain for the early settlers. The multitude in the mainstream lack the courage or risk-taking ability to lead it.

However, since the mainstream is much more subject to trendiness than its members recognize, policymakers can influence its flow through media images. Only when the media reflect what early settlers have already done, does the mainstream shift course, whether into new hair lengths, fashions, or lifestyles.

Stragglers come last in the neighborhood dynamics, which increasingly sift and sort household types, after most of the turnover is complete. Their arrival already may spur the previous comers to move on.

The estimates of aggregate population change are tentative. Admittedly the typology needs to be refined and tested in more cities, but it can serve policymakers as a guide to the identification of the stages of gentrification.

Speculation.   Speculation strictly means engaging in risky investments for quick and considerable profit, but many consider anyone making money in housing a speculator. In regions where neighborhood values were sharply discounted, and rediscovery is only the opening trickle in a surge of new urban housing demand, there will be substantial windfall gains unless supply coming on the market can be expanded to match demand.

Where newcomers differ substantially from traditional replacement buyers, existing residents are likely to suspect speculation even on the part of resident owners. Such strains are revealed by looking at revitalization through the eyes of its long-term residents. Prior to the arrival of newcomers, the incumbents have often accepted that their neighborhood is on the downgrade, and no longer worth investing in. Even if not actually red-lined, paying 12 percent interest on home improvement loans seems highway robbery to them. The more sophisticated newcomers, less concerned about unemployment, see even a 10 percent mortgage as bearing effectively no interest in these inflationary times. To them the $40,000 urban home has both greater appreciation potential and less financial exposure than the $100,000 suburban alternative. This is an ironic new twist to the massive suburban flight away from urban problems of past decades. What newcomers felt was a difficult housing decision may already be called speculation by existing residents.

As the self-fulfilling decline syndrome is turned around, speculation may now erupt. A slight excess of buyers attracts other buyers and encourages some sellers to hold on. The more complexity obscures the housing market, the more speculation is fueled.

As the media show urban rediscovery of brownstones and incipient Georgetowns, excessive demand develops, inflating property values. When the tax collector begins to assess all property (not just those sold) at these new values, higher taxes fall on existing residents who remain. Without appropriate intervention displacement occurs, as speculation feeds on itself. And as particular owners seek ways to capture the excessive demand, investment motives begin to replace homeownership. Greed moves in next to need. Basements become garden apartments, attics and garages become lofts and carriage house apartments. Arson can occur to remove the disadvantaged, as documented in revitalizing sections of Philadelphia and around the Mission District BART Station in San Francisco.

Through many different scenarios, the incentives that promote good maintenance in stable markets collapse with the prospect of gains. Since turnover and displacement are necessary to obtain these gains, policy should focus on dealing with the impact of turnover.

Stable Markets

It is only in stable areas, where demand is steady and predictable, that natural forces still normalize behavior and check deterioration. Only here does housing appear to maintain itself, the good properties visibly doing better than the worse ones. Here homeostasis still governs. In contrast, investments in improvements in weak markets usually no longer repay themselves, while in high demand areas there is a market for everything regardless of condition. The process of incumbent upgrading illustrates how stability can be maintained through sensitive public planning.

Upgrading. Upgrading by incumbents results when the residents reappraise their situation and decide they gain more satisfaction by improving the housing where they already live than by moving elsewhere. This complex choice is a function of countless factors including costs of desired improvements, costs of moving, image of the neighborhood, continued suitability of the stock, as well as taking into account what others in the neighborhood are doing.

The critical difference between upgrading and gentrification or decline lies in the residents' sense of predictability and control of the neighborhood's future. Upgrading is likely where turnover replaces departing owners with newcomers whom the residents view as good neighbors. The prevalence of normal upgrading has become obscured by the media and political preoccupations with areas of noteworthy population change. However, such upgrading is actively being promoted by the Federal Home Loan Banks, and many cities are developing visible models in Neighborhood Housing Services.

Incumbent upgrading can best be understood by considering Pittsburgh's Neighborhood Housing Services (PNHS), now in the process of being copied in scores of cities under the influence of the federal Urban Reinvestment Task Force (URTF). PNHS began with Ford Foundation-funded grass roots organizing to build neighborhood confidence, fight encroaching large-scale absentee owners, and challenge the private sector to offer credit. The resulting nonprofit technical assistance corporation has a board composed of lenders and community representatives, who have a slight majority. Here public sector code enforcement has become effective. An imaginative special loan fund was created by PNHS to assist those who could not afford conventional loans for home improvements, while the code enforcement process was tailored so that renovation was within the financial grasp of the majority of area residents. As residents saw the area improve, they willingly met modest monthly increased housing costs. Property values appreciated appropriately, making recovery of the outlays from the special loan fund possible when the properties of households on restricted incomes are eventually sold.

The public policy key lies in matching housing demand with supply. This approach allows those who wish to remain to be subsidized equitably. The return of confidence is somehow signaled to the network of participants who all have roles in maintaining the neighborhood. Whereas in the surge of gentrification various interests become disarrayed or polarized, in this type of upgrading PHNS was able to communicate confidence to the residents as well as to many in the public and private sectors who were in the process of writing off this area. This coordinated every participant's behavior—improving municipal services, restructuring code enforcement, and revising lending underwriting criteria. As homeostasis was restored the change here was comprehensive and beneficial to all.

HOW PREVALENT ARE THESE VARIOUS MARKETS?

It is impossible to tell how many dwelling units are currently in declining, rising, and stable markets until the research proposed in Chapter 3 is done because there are neither standards nor data. But it is already clear that three factors, in decreasing order of importance, must be considered in providing the answer.

First, the proportion of stock that is declining, rising, and stable in any particular city is a function of the contextual factors identified in Chapter 4. Just as West Coast cities reflect their growth in a greater proportion of rising neighborhoods, the stagnation or decline affecting parts of the Northeast is reflected in more neighborhoods experiencing disinvestment and even outright abandonment.

Second, demand and supply must be disaggregated and analyzed separately. The constraints that may prevent supply from responding to changing effective demand are important to identify and overcome. In some Midwest cities where prairies are still being turned into subdivisions there recently has been overbuilding, causing abandonment. In California, on the other hand, tight land use controls have prevented enough new construction, leading to incredible inflation in housing values and outright speculation. Further, in examining demand more closely, it makes a great difference whether the demand originates from elderly or young traditional households, or students and young professionals prone to new lifestyles. Each has its own significance.

Third, at an even finer level of detail, a host of factors comes into play. Where matters have become too complex, the media simplify and interpret the role of these factors, which include the local school system, tax and crime rates, the central city's share of the metropolitan area, type of government, housing stock composition, and the like. However, in spite of current planners' preoccupation with these factors, perhaps due to the media, they appear dwarfed in importance by the above.

SUMMARY

In complex urban systems feedback on market change is increasingly erratic. Areas that have begun to experience revitalization are often still perceived as declining by most private institutions and city officials. In spite of Sunday magazine supplement articles focused on house tours and stories about young households fixing up structures in particular neighborhoods, in many cities key officials are often only dimly aware of the implications of these trends or dubious that potentially significant changes are actually underway. They still classify such areas as declining. This variance in different participants' perceptions plays a key role.

First, insufficient effective housing demand or difficulties in obtaining credit allow neighborhood image and values to decline to the point where houses become real opportunities for those who can figure out how to purchase them. This attracts pioneers to move in. Then various housing participants develop conflicting perceptions of the same neighborhood. This leads pioneers and early settlers to work extremely hard to develop a new neighborhood image, and often involves a new name for the neighborhood undergoing revitalization. Absolute numbers of new households moving in are less significant than whatever dissonance is generated between newcomers and existing residents, which attracts the media. If people then remark on their differences, it makes waves. Media publicity focused on this revival opens a floodgate of new demand. The multitude of baby-boom households currently forming, with owners who assumed they would buy in new suburban subdivisions only to discover them unaffordable, thereby glimpse a whole new set of options.

Many of these urban neighborhoods are now bargains waiting to be discovered, but existing residents and most policymakers do not see them that way. Energy concerns and new women's career and employment patterns are bringing large numbers of new household types into the urban market with higher disposable incomes, fewer children, and less current concern about child-raising, yards, and schools. Few have as yet recognized how great a premium these new household types would place on being nearer the action if norms and status permit. All of this translates into a radical shift in traditional housing demand patterns, and for some urban neighborhoods this can mean a sharp, unexpected resurgence in demand, taking local officials by surprise. By then it will be more difficult for them to realize that stable markets are ideal while rapidly rising markets are likely to overheat. The planners' role is to match supply with demand and to prevent unexpected shifts that destroy homeostasis. The complexity compounded by the myopia of special interests makes this a formidable challenge.

The media increasingly focus everyone's preoccupations in this drama, letting the big picture slip from view. With this in mind, it seems time to discover a more constructive role for media influence.

Chapter 7

Media Images of Neighborhoods

As complexity increasingly obscures urban property values, media perceptions orchestrate the factors that determine value. Because the media pervade national and local actions their impact is difficult to recognize, but using it to influence neighborhood perception has already been discovered by some cities as an effective planning tool. Such boosterism can confer benefits; but if used irresponsibly, it can just as easily prove detrimental to the public welfare.

In a number of U.S. cities a new kind of neighborhood promotion has recently emerged. Seattle broadcast thirty-second television images developed around such themes as "If you lived here, you'd be home now!" (and not still caught in traffic). In 1972, some resident Boston planners began with a slide show called "So you thought you knew Dorchester!" that was then turned into an eye-catching poster by the neighborhood planning staff. It stressed overlooked neighborhood opportunities such as Victorian houses, good location, ocean views, and beaches. The request of a local bank for several thousand copies to reward depositors who opened new accounts or made a substantial deposit told the planners they were on to something. (Local bank leadership, challenged for red-lining, sought many means of improving community relations).

An English and Spanish poster on Jamaica Plain followed, to help another red-lined community. This one was designed by the neighborhood planning staff to accompany the prime time, upbeat television special mentioned in Chapter 4.

A Roxbury poster was then designed with community input. Two brochures aimed at a wider audience have also been produced: one on Boston's triple-deckers and the other on "Living in Boston," which individually reviews the attributes of each neighborhood. (Rugo, 1979)

Initially such boosterism was considered by many seasoned urban planners as naive, but it preceded a remarkable amount of neighborhood reinvestment. Attitudes of existing residents toward their homes also became more positive. Condition data and citizen attitude surveys quickly reflected this. Many also sought the posters out of nostalgia, welcoming a change from the negative press image that seemed to have enveloped the neighborhoods in which they grew up. How can policymakers judge the appropriateness of such boosterism? They need to see it in context.

A BRIEF HISTORY OF CHANGING
NEIGHBORHOOD SELF-IMAGE

Clearly a throw-away mentality had been allowed to permeate most perceptions of urban neighborhoods. "New" became equated with "better." Old Dutch Cleanser, an effective, age-old scouring powder, tried in the 1960s to become NEW Old Dutch Cleanser but did not survive. At that time the future of urban neighborhoods looked little better. Federal assistance applications required stressing all the negative attributes: abandonment, dilapidation, and even "poverty counted twice." Statement of these negative factors determined the amount of assistance any urban neighborhood would get.

A city like Boston with a residential stock worth billions of dollars was compelled to bad-mouth itself to obtain mere millions of dollars of federal Urban Renewal, Model Cities, and housing assistance. As the media reported these efforts, confidence throughout the city ebbed.

News, by definition, is not the norm, but increasing complexity permits the sensational, or newsworthy, to become confused with the norm. The focus of the media on such events allows underlying changes to escape detection. A low income housing corporation rehabilitating thirteen dwellings is human interest news, and planners became preoccupied with facilitating such events, giving little thought to the many different impressions this would generate.

It is doubtful any policymakers tried to match up overall rates of change in the number of households with actual growth and changes in the metropolitan housing stock, particularly new starts in suburban subdivisions. However, in most northeast metropolitan areas they would have discovered that an overproduction of housing during the 1960s and early 1970s was spurred by FHA-facilitated credit. Overproduction was a significant contributor to general discouragement with the urban predicament. It was probably more of a genuine cause of abandonment than the federal urban initiatives were a genuine solution. This never made the news.

Now an era of scarce housing has dawned in the majority of metropolitan areas, yet equally few appear to recognize the new implications. As growth controls and environmental concerns constrain production nearly everywhere, housing costs are soaring out of sight. This not only refocuses demand into previously overlooked neighborhoods but, since the stock market does not seem to keep pace with inflation, it is also compounded with demand from nonresident investors who now show more interest in urban housing. Needing only modest equity, many can play with housing futures like speculators in scarce commodities.

Media coverage fails to coherently relate continuing abandonment, inflation, the baby bulge, urban rediscovery, federal urban policy, and speculation. Yet their interrelationships are essential to understand before intervention.

TOO MANY HOUSING ROLES OBSCURE THE MARKET

When it is no longer clear what determines property values, past economic models become not only useless but misleading. Economics posits an invisible hand that matches supply with demand. Many housing market imperfections are acknowledged, but that housing demand declines as the cost of housing increases is still considered axiomatic. Only a few can afford expensive housing, while more buyers appear when the price drops. From the buyer's viewpoint, if housing costs too much in one area, he will buy in another area where he will get better value for his dollar. This logic assumes the buyer can independently judge value.

Many have unconsciously slipped through the looking glass into a counterintuitive world where it is unclear what determines value: If everyone is selecting houses over here, this area must be better in status; and if it is so much cheaper over there, something must be wrong and that area acquires a stigma.

Consider Mr. and Mrs. Urbane who really wanted an urban Victorian structure in 1970, but could not obtain credit for it. So instead they bought what Mr. Urbane now calls "a lifetime of mortgage payments for a jerry-built ticky-tacky box in a far-out suburban subdivision." The broker, lender, and appraiser all seemed part of a closed system to warn him that if he bought the urban Victorian, he would be a dunce, unable to sell it when he realized what he had done.

But the urban Victorian, bought by another with independent financing, has now tripled in value, outperforming the ticky-tacky box. All the secondary actors within the housing system—brokers, lenders, and appraisers—took no risks themselves, assumed continued obsolescence, ignored the settling down of the postwar baby bulge, and did not realize that outside investment might rapidly drive up values in older neighborhoods after the bicentennial. Few could have predicted how these shifts would compound, but in hindsight the Urbanes feel they should have been free to take these risks rather than to have simply been red-lined. Urban residents who saw their neighborhoods decline because willing replacement buyers were unable to find financing agree with the Urbanes.

At any point in time, each urban neighborhood has its place in the metropolitan system. Its accessibility, demographics, and housing conditions, as well as quality and cost of services, can be considered as given by the past. Its change can be viewed as resulting from an ecology with countless interactions among residents, sellers, and buyers. Its rich complexity can only be glimpsed by any one participant. Each individual acts from his perception of self-interest, which has been shaped by cultural conditioning. All these actions aggregate into market behavior—buying and selling, investing, maintaining, upgrading, converting, speculating, disinvesting, abandoning, demolishing, and rebuilding. All this behavior in turn feeds back into neighborhood conditions—adding, improving, or subtracting housing, altering accessibility, and enhancing or tarnishing this neighborhood's ranking among its competitors in the region. The vitality of the entire system is threatened when parts are closed off, as, for example, when brokers, lenders, and appraisers short-circuited the Urbane's choices.

Figure 7–1 sketches this feedback dynamic and lists the actors and roles involved. Obviously this system embraces a wide range of potential participants—a range that can expand or contract. When turnover increases, for example, more residents become sellers and more buyers must be found to fill the vacated units. If there is a lack of buyers or willing lenders for any neighborhood, then conditions are likely to deteriorate.

A few persons can share a wealth of information among themselves. As their numbers increase, the amount of information that can be shared sharply declines and misinterpretations become more likely. The future of such neighborhoods now involves a growing

Figure 7–1. Feedback Between Neighborhood Conditions and Market Behavior

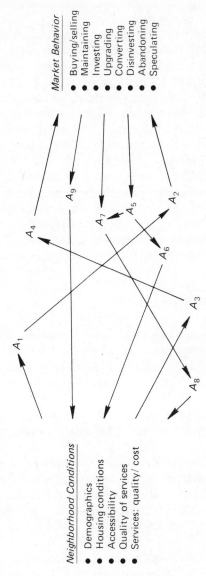

Market Behavior

- Buying/selling
- Maintaining
- Investing
- Upgrading
- Converting
- Disinvesting
- Abandoning
- Speculating

Neighborhood Conditions

- Demographics
- Housing conditions
- Accessibility
- Quality of services
- Services: quality/cost

$A_{1 \ldots n}$ = *Countless Market Actors*
each having independent
perceptions of the market
and his or her self-interest:

- Sellers, potential sellers
- Buyers, potential buyers
- Brokers, potential brokers
- Appraisers
- Lenders
- Investors
- Contractors
- Public servants

network of roles. Increasing complexity makes this future much more vulnerable to misunderstandings. The urban participants now include a growing host of public officials, along with residents, potential buyers, brokers, appraisers, lenders and insurers, outside investors, property managers, and the like.

In the past the neighborhood's natural ecology maintained its own stability and induced all to play their appropriate parts in maintaining the neighborhood. The behavior of each of these actors was traditionally shaped by the information passing among them. Now as neighborhood confidence and self-image fluctuate in uncertainty, "wait and see" and looking for housing elsewhere have become prudent alternatives to simply continuing to act. With many more roles and as reality becomes obscured by more and more political promises, it is easy to expect that "someone else should do it."

As this diffusion of responsibility compounds with the postwar tendency toward anticipating obsolescence, seeking the new and discarding the old, many of the urban participants have unconsciously become joined in a self-fulfilling syndrome of disinvesting. Many realize that the Urbanes were not well-advised while the "dunce" who bought the urban Victorian did well. However, there is confusion as to what to expect next.

THE MEDIA EMERGE TO ORCHESTRATE THE HOUSING ROLES

Within this forum containing too many roles but too little communication, the media have emerged as a decisive influence. The media can project a pessimistic neighborhood image, discouraging urban housing demand. Then, unexpected positive images can trigger an overreaction as speculatively inclined short-term investors come in to make matters worse. Figure 7–2 suggests how this focusing role is played by the media.

A simple media statement saying that there is block-busting in a neighborhood or that the elderly residents are unable to maintain their homes properly leads to a chain reaction. More residents will then try to sell their homes before it is too late, just as potential replacement buyers will decide to give this neighborhood a wide berth. Prices can plummet.

At the other extreme, stories about enthusiastic pioneers rediscovering Victorian structures spur many to try to join an uplifting market, just as residents reconsider and decide to remain. The media are difficult to fine tune. Follow-up news of the discovery leads to excessive market pressure. Prices soar as too many bid for the few

Figure 7-2. Media Interpret Neighborhood Conditions and Influence Market Behavior

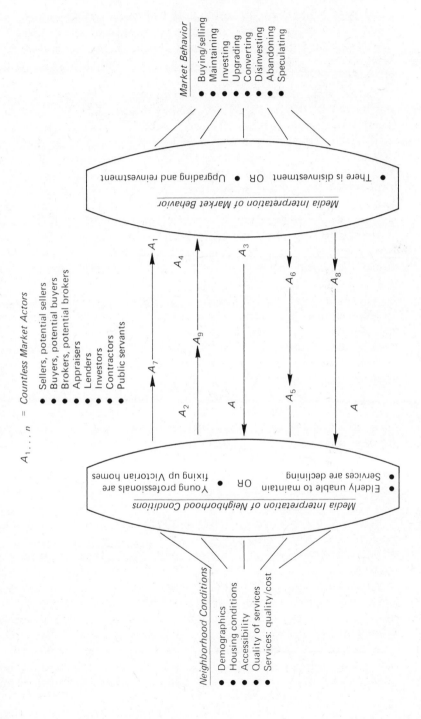

properties that reach the market. If the media say there is displacement—something no one can agree on how to measure—then many accept without question that this condition is present and cannot be altered. Even judging the desirability of these conditions is left to the media.

Participants normally carry incomplete, out-dated, and conflicting images of the future of any neighborhood. Market situations normally handle that; errors cancel out or self-correct to a large degree. The media, however, cannot broadcast everyone's viewpoint—there would be neither time nor interest for that. The media must be selective, yet selecting certain voices mutes the others. In this selection process the simple and sensational has the edge over questioning and probing uncertainties. High officials such as a bank president or mayor are invited to state neighborhood concerns when a resident, a loan officer, or a neighborhood planner may actually be much better informed and may have actually briefed the higher official. Special interests acting through sponsors, station managers, or licensing boards may force editing.

The legitimacy of the resulting printed or broadcast messages is more real than life, more authoritative in influence than any actual human interaction. This is particularly true in anomic and high turnover neighborhoods where firsthand experience plays a lesser role.

The images now focused and projected by the media influence a great many participants' assessments, often damaging or short-circuiting the delicate ecology of individual motivations that have maintained neighborhoods in the past. Evidence of the loss of homeostasis appears only well after the balance has been upset. Media images have developed an unrecognized influence in determining the futures of marginal neighborhoods. It is natural that most industry spokesmen would deny such impact, yet even when the industry intended to produce the opposite effect, media coverage tended to exacerbate dynamics.

Who knows what images are created in the minds of hearers and viewers? Abandonment may be a serious issue but showing empty structures in a thirty-second news item to call attention to the city's inability to deal effectively with the situation makes matters worse. Even if the city demolishes the exposed buildings immediately, many more structures become at risk when the news convinces brokers, residents, and potential buyers that the neighborhood is suffering from terminal illness.

Awareness of racial change in Hyde Park, a formerly all-white section of Boston, sharpened in August 1976 when the media broadcast allegations of blockbusting. This prompted a wave of discretionary turnover, as previously undecided homeowners decided to sell. Then at a meeting in late August, city officials, brokers, and media representatives discussed the potential counterintuitive reactions even balanced reporting of the situation had produced. As further news coverage ceased, turnover again slowed to a rate acceptable to most residents. Given the agitated state of the city concerning school busing and classroom assignments for desegregation, having no media coverage was most effective in maintaining the neighborhood because this allowed homeostasis to prevail.

This discussion began with the economic axiom that a home buyer was an independent judge of value, supported in his choice by real estate intermediaries. Increased complexity and uncertainty have obscured the process of determining value to the point where the multitude, out of uncertainty, seek an impartial arbiter of value. They have adopted the media to play that role. As media images replace firsthand experience and alter mass behavior, neighborhood markets are swept by unprecedented ebbs and flows of demand.

Neighborhood boosterism joins with these complex dynamics, drawing housing further into a realm in which the huckster and speculator have long been at home.

WHERE CAN ONE GO FROM HERE?

Clearly, one might seek to restore the simple world in which housing is judged on its merits by each buyer, with lenders and appraisers simply checking the buyer's value judgment. A restored faith in the future of urban neighborhoods, along with proper bank credit, might restore homeostasis and induce upgrading.

However, it seems that increased complexity and recent public interventions have already unbalanced many urban markets too far. In the tidal wave of new households, some seek to settle in tight metropolitan markets. They are followed by others. In the absence of intervention they are likely to select choice neighborhoods. There they bring about new enclaves through rapid population transfusion, displacing and scattering previous residents through escalating housing prices. This is news, and the most dramatic views get spliced into thirty seconds for the nightly news.

How can neighborhood media images be improved without deranging the system further and inducing fresh speculation in enclaves within a context of continuing urban disinvestment? The only recourse for policymakers is to understand the supply/demand imbalances throughout their region, correct them as best they can, and then to work in partnership with the media. The traditional urban

planning tools like rental assistance, below market interest mortgages, and subsidized construction are almost useless, like pebbles in
these new demographic tides. However, the currents are favorable to
such new urban revitalization initiatives as spreading the new demand
around to neighborhoods in less demand. Done properly, this en-
hances the value of overlooked but not obsolete stock types and prevents speculation.

INFLUENCING NEIGHBORHOOD
DEMAND THROUGH MEDIA IMAGES

Planners tend to seek direct influence, but indirect approaches are
most effective. People do not necessarily buy where they are told to
buy. Although hidden cultural traits and complex rationalizations
mask actual decisionmaking, people believe they make their own
choices after rationally considering many alternatives. Automotive
market research found that many American car buyers actually seek
powerful new sex symbols every few years and do not expect them
to last (instead of requiring energy efficient, long-lasting vehicles).
Similar investigations should examine the housing selection process
more rigorously. Research conducted at the Boston Redevelopment
Authority (BRA) into how residential selections are actually made
suggests that to be thought smart now seems as important as pursuing a rational economic calculus. No one wants to be thought a
dunce and many will apparently pay substantially to avoid making
what others consider a poor selection.

When people with choices, that is, those more experienced or with
more education, are seen selecting or endorsing a particular neighborhood, this boosts the confidence of those already there and in turn
strengthens the demand for the neighborhood. This principle can
guide rebuilding neighborhood pride. "Breakfast of Champions"
illustrates this principle applied to food. Housing is more difficult.
One can make more Wheaties, but a neighborhood is both finite and
extraordinarily sensitive to supply/demand imbalances. Residents
want the neighborhood to be recognized as a good place to live, yet
they neither want to be displaced nor have their housing costs go up.
To restore urban neighborhood self-image, the media can help focus
on the positive attributes of each, producing a sincere "I'm O.K.,
you're O.K." for neighborhoods.

Some examples provide a good beginning for discussion. Consider
Where's Boston? This fifty-minute, multi-image audio-visual show
was prepared for the Bicentennial to give visitors a better appreciation of Boston heritage and a positive feeling for the city today. It

was so successful that it is still shown continuously at a theater in downtown Boston. Within its kaleidoscope came not only historic buildings, the Tall Ships under sail, Quen Elizabeth's visit, Yankee dowagers, Boston Brahmins, and Arthur Fiedler's Fourth of July celebration on the Esplanade, but every ethnic group in Boston's potpourri. The result was a rare, moving experience that not only impressed visitors but induced residents to see it again and to take their friends—in effect, to show them Boston much as one shows off a Polaroid self-portrait. *Where's Boston?* helped everyone feel proud and put the agonizing media coverage of Boston's resistance to busing into perspective.

Other examples of positive media coverage include recent Sunday supplement articles tracing the history of some neighborhoods, chronicling black achievements, and describing the positive outlook of immigrants moving to Boston from the Caribbean, Cape Verde, Greece, and Ireland today. TV and life style sections have shown glimpses of young residents making unheralded but imaginative changes in Boston's triple deckers. Such media efforts convey a positive feeling, helping the readers and viewers appreciate how others shape their lives in a pluralistic urban society.

These bridging efforts stand in constructive contrast to conventional media reporting of urban crime, failing public services, declining reading achievement scores, and white flight, all of which polarize attitudes. As this conventional coverage draws caricatures, it renders those in the suburbs more smug and feeling thankful it does not happen there. But it also inadvertently portrays the urban predicament as so discouraging that all who have any option avoid it. Those without any choice become frantic or simply resigned.

Advertisers prize the persuasive immediacy of the media. The industry seems to have failed to recognize how these same qualities pervade all coverage. Casual judgments appear final and irrefutable. As long as insensitive coverage persists in interpreting the news through obsolescing stereotyped images, the homeostasis that shaped behavior and stabilized neighborhoods in the past will remain suspended or crippled. Unless the conventional media approach to the urban predicament alters, the damage will be enormous.

Media oversimplifications have become suspect. The urban scene is not all that dreadful and the suburbs are not all that great. This realization frees many to express hidden attitudes, and human interest stories can capture their views.

The media can also foster housing demand in neighborhoods less popular, and reveal overlooked opportunities. A homebuying scenario illustrates this.

The Welches have decided that the time has come to settle down. They want to know what kind of housing people like themselves are choosing. Both directly and indirectly, newspaper stories and television programs strongly shape what places they will consider. After a television program or remarks from acquaintances raised their interest in a particular location, they clip news articles on housing costs, on the pros and cons of different locations, and on how renovations and imaginative redesign can be handled. Such clippings may also be shown to them by a real estate broker to whom they have turned after their interest was sparked. At the back of their minds is the question, Are people there like us?

If the images they have encountered so far are inconsistent, they will try to meet actual residents, attend a house tour or garage sale. These common events provide further constructive opportunities for media communications, if handled with sensitivity to avoid the dynamics of gentrification.

Many residents are photogenic and can tell something interesting about themselves in virtually all neighborhoods. Such images help neighborhoods regain their confidence when the past impression was that only problems existed.

The Boston media have willingly provided such people with access to news time and space. Neighborhood planners initially played a matchmaking role in helping residents find appropriate media exposure, but soon this innovative approach took hold and became more spontaneous (Rugo, 1979). This process, in turn, brought about a new tone in urban media coverage. Reporters already residing in urban areas, who previously had not found the courage to speak out alone, now found access to the editorial pages. As more reporters moved into urban neighborhoods, media coverage perceptibly improved and neighborhood slurs declined.

"This Old House," a fourteen-week spring 1979 television production has been nick-named the Julia Child of home repair. The program, which focused on a deteriorating but attractive small Victorian house in a weak neighborhood, is another illustration of the rich possibilities open to the media for revealing hidden facets of weaker urban neighborhoods.

The Boston partnership with the media has become very creative and constructive. As a result, there are now many articles and frequent television items that show the Welches that people like them live happily in urban neighborhoods. When the Welches mention to friends and acquaintances that they are considering buying a two-family house in Jamaica Plain or Dorchester, their friends are interested and supportive, *and think them smart*. Only five years ago the

Urbanes thought they would have been looked upon as mad. What changed? The turning point in conventional reactions was signalled when the CBS evening news with Walter Cronkite spent four minutes of national prime time talking with understanding about Boston's South End and Dorchester. Since this broadcast so effectively addressed many common concerns, it is transcribed below.

CBS Evening News, Friday, December 9, 1977

Walter Cronkite: The White House already is working on President Carter's first State of the Union speech next month, and CBS News has learned that he's considering proposing new aid to financially troubled big cities. It would include tax breaks to encourage investment and loans to companies that build factories and create jobs in the inner city. There may be another encouraging development for the cities whose tax bases long have been eroded by migration of the middle-class to the suburbs. Bruce Morton has gone to Boston for that story.

Bruce Morton: This was the pattern for generations. Middle-class kids grew up, got married, bought a house in the suburbs. Many still do. But some young people in some neighborhoods are making a different choice: buying and rehabilitating older housing in the city.

Frank and Polly Smith bought here on Dwight Street in Boston's South End three and a half years ago. They put about $20,000 and a lot of time and sweat into fixing up their hundred year old house. They like city living, with qualifications. Polly misses greenery, but finds crime less of a problem than she might have expected.

Polly Smith: This particular part of the South End has been remarkably free of crime. There have been some incidents recently, but for the most part we've been very fortunate I think. And people feel safe here, and pretty much have a sense of who belongs on the street, and feel good about living here.

Bruce Morton: The older of your children is two, I think, and that means that in two or three years she'll be going to school. What do you think about the public schools? Would that make you stay in the South End, or make you want to leave, or what?

Frank Smith: It's probably the biggest problem that people like us face, not only in the South End but citywide. People who want to come into the city and raise a family and yet have certain expectations as to what type of academic experience their kids are going to have. I don't know what we'll end up doing.

Bruce Morton: It is not, the experts say, that people are abandoning the suburbs. What's happened instead is that the baby boom generation, born just after World War II, has reached home buying age, drastically expanding the market. And there are more households than there used to be, fewer big families, more childless couples, more singles. For a variety of reasons some of these people are choosing to live in the cities.

Gael Jose and her husband, who are refurbishing this big old Victorian frame house in Dorchester, like it, she says, because it is more fun than the little town where she grew up.

Gael Jose: Living in a small town was a little stifling, and I felt isolated, whereas here in the city there's always something to do. There's all kinds of cultural and sporting events and lots of different kinds of people to meet and talk to.

Bruce Morton: The new city folks cite various reasons for their choice. More house for the money, some of these Victorian frame giants are only $30,000 or so, and a little repair work can make that a sound investment. No commuting—city dwellers may be a short subway ride or even a walk from work. Fashion—some inner city neighborhoods are becoming chic. And finally, the lure of city life—culture, shops, churches, and some things you just don't find in the suburbs. (Film of one man band at Quincy Market.)

The rehabilitation of city neighborhoods is mostly a private phenomenon, but cities can encourage it. Boston has spent $500,000,000 on amenities like parks and playgrounds. And the new city dwellers are not a mass movement. Other people are still leaving. Buildings are still abandoned. Both things happening at once. Mayor Kevin White says the newcomers are a blessing, sort of.

Kevin White: A blessing and a burden, Bruce, it comes in both forms. One, you bring people in: it's jobs, it's vitality, it stimulates, the city's alive. And psychologically, it's good for the city. But they will want more schools, better streets, and put different demands. So there's a balance. Obviously I would opt for the inflow, and in the long run it's probably on one of the best signs for the cities in the last, probably, six or seven decades.

Bruce Morton: There are problems. Will the new arrivals displace the older city residents? Especially the poor? The experts say what they lack are good statistics. They don't know how big the move to the cities is or will become. They do say that, whatever its size, it's good news.

© 1977 CBS Inc.

Before this broadcast those who had bought homes in Dorchester saw themselves as courageous pioneers but said little about it, and were used to long distance calls from concerned relatives, parents, and even friends in their own generation. Subsequently, the previously undecided felt they knew all-along it was going to turn out all right. Demand firmed as risks were put in a new perspective. As prices moved up from the low $20,000s to the high $30,000s, the pioneers were seen as simply lucky to have arrived there first.

Here the media played a constructive role, restoring vitality to a weak housing market. But today, as the same properties are rising in value to the $50,000s, more media coverage would heat speculation. It is time to redirect such endorsements to weaker neighborhoods by enabling residents there too to project infectious enthusiasm.

In summary, the media can as easily inform, encourage, and educate as discourage the public about this urban frontier. The key lies in developing an awareness of what is beneficial to neighborhood stability and discovering how to produce more of it. Herein lies a new partnership between policymakers and corporate interests.

Few now recognize the awesome influence of the media, but as soon as more people do, it will be time to consider how urban hucksterism can be checked. If the media are used in marketing urban neighborhoods Madison Avenue style, insensitive to their flaws, then the beneficial opportunities the media afford will be swept away by cynical resistance or even more regulations. This media approach is only effective in restoring the image of basically attractive urban neighborhoods that have been maligned and thus become tarnished and neglected. It so happens this includes the majority of our urban neighborhoods.

Chapter 8

The Federal Magic Show
and Neighborhood Initiatives

A sizable gap has developed between the expectations of the disadvantaged and the resources society is willing to commit to fulfill those expectations. Politicians are elected to lead the public toward meeting these urgent needs, but they do not know the way. Bureaucrats are expected to design and carry out the programs that address the needs, but they only know the available resources are inadequate. These policymaking partners neither reveal the inadequacy of means nor attempt to scale down the public's expectations. They begin by supporting what seems promising.

Innovative community actions are frequently granted federal support as "replicable models" and "breakthroughs" in changing the system. As soon as heralded, the promising initiatives themselves often become transformed instead, as if federal support had an inverse Midas touch, turning them to clay. How does this come about? What is required to maintain the promise of true community initiatives? Consider two examples.

Adopt-a-Building represents a community-initiated, privately financed takeover of owner-abandoned tenements by Spanish-speaking lower East Side tenants. Because their past owners and managers found that New York's tangle of restrictions, rent controls, and tax laws had eroded all their self-interest in continuing to own and manage these properties, they abandoned them. Thereupon, the tenants took over 519 East 11th Street and began fix-up. Necessity led them to innovate. Several New York officials cut some of the red tape to help their efforts and they were simply able to ignore other laws.

When the promise of restoring this housing was evident, federal assistance entered the picture to add rooftop solar collector panels, hydroponic gardens, and windmill power, and to broadcast the success of this tenant initiative through the national media. HUD also provided substantial rental assistance, but this also meant paying higher union scale wages (required under the Davis-Bacon Act), and even more red tape. Once the Adopt-a-Building approach was in the limelight, ignoring the red tape jungle became much more difficult. Inspired improvisations were not enough to revitalize New York tenements. Instead they have turned into a complex federal/community collaboration known as the Urban Homesteading Assistance Board projects, or U–HAB.

The Charlotte Street project in the South Bronx is another example. This area was visited by President Jimmy Carter and HUD Secretary Patricia Harris after it had become the national symbol of the failure of past urban policies. Here, too, long before this federal visit, a dedicated team of local individuals was grappling on its own with the immense problems of revitalizing the South Bronx. After the visit by the President, HUD seems to have been pressured. It has hired master-planner Ed Logue to produce new, assisted housing on the very spot where the top federal housing officials met with community representatives. The specifications call for pulling a rabbit out of a hat.

PUTTING THESE EFFORTS IN PERSPECTIVE

While these instances of revitalization can at best restore 1,000 dwelling units annually, New York housing statistics suggest that 27,000 housing units, no longer considered worth maintaining by private entrepreneurs, are currently going the other way through tax delinquency to city/ownership. However, it seems the public wants to believe in these creative neighborhood initiatives. To them they offer promise that through replication of their example the urban predicament will be transformed, enabling many more disadvantaged groups to attain decent housing.

These are but two examples presented at an issue forum focused on successes in dealing with the problems of distressed, urban, multifamily properties. This forum was convened by the National Commission on Neighborhoods and held at the prestigious Ford Foundation headquarters in New York City, in June 1978. The two days of the forum were dominated by inspiring personal accounts by leaders of disadvantaged community groups. This forum suggested that policymakers mesmerize the public, the technical experts, and ultimately themselves by facilitating such limited efforts.

HUD's presence at the forum was palpable, discreetly assisting in the presentation. The community initiators seemed to be on show as role models for others to emulate: David's versus New York's Goliath bureaucracy. Can more Davids be created? Is that really a solution?

Better communication would have resulted at the forum if individuals other than the principal participants outlined each effort, and the participants themselves were introduced to answer questions, fill in details, and elaborate only where necessary. For some reason this approach was rejected. Why did most of the participants at the forum see the efforts as heroic and shy away from putting these achievements into a broader context?

The listeners were clearly divided into two groups. The literalists, those fascinated by the intricacies of how the federal and state tools were actually employed (tax-exempt bond-financing, compounded with write downs, federal subsidies, local tax concessions, and the like), were clearly the majority. There were only a sprinkling of generalists—those concerned with the bigger picture (how these individual efforts to rehabilitate relate to overall urban dynamics in size and impact). Why was the quixotic nature of these efforts not apparent to all?

This forum seemed part of a complex deception that had already mesmerized most of the participants. What an uncomfortable thought! Through persistence, ignoring some laws and having others waived, these efforts by disadvantaged community groups are succeeding. With similar waivers, many of the 27,000 units would not be in trouble either.

New York's basic problem is red tape blight, which strangles too many normal incentives to maintain housing. The climate clearly violates the Housing Policy Law developed in Chapter 5. A complex maze of laws, administrative regulations, and bureaucracy prevents ordinary owners from seeing a fair return on their efforts. This leads them to abandon property. Instead of determining how the overall complexity and uncertainty can be reduced to the point where normal maintenance of housing resumes, recognition is now given to heroic but futile efforts to overcome complexity. One knows that recognition is being given to an illusion when one realizes that the bureaucrats regularly arrange waivers or help only certain initiatives overcome the red tape while it is left intact for all others.

These initiatives will not change the overall laws and regulations. They are decoys provided so the laws are left intact. Nor will these

initiatives serve as prototypes whose high per unit costs can be re-
covered through economies of scale in reproduction. Much hidden
effort and many subsidies have been expended to produce these
blooms in the desert. "Pump-priming" and "system change" are only
misleading euphemisms for such costly demonstrations. The individual actors are unaware of their role in the dominant system, which
produces the urban predicament and which now also misleads with
these illusions of change.

WHAT CREATES THE SLEIGHT OF HAND?

Focusing the national media spotlight on the plight of the disadvantaged sets up complex dynamics. Many who know nothing of the
South Bronx and even less about what has taken place there interpret
the plight of the residents as a national disgrace. Once this desert is
shown on prime time television, the public sector appears charged to
make it bloom, and the audience simply seems to thirst for a mirage.

The disadvantaged, on the other hand, are also moved by complex
motivations. Needing help, they know television exposure can gal-
vanize the will to act in ways no letters to the president and no calls
to their Congressman ever can. In the third world, the saying is "If
you're starving, don't do it in the bush, but on the palace steps—
you're more likely to get help." Television provides a modern counterpart to the palace steps.

The individuals acting in this drama are only human, but they
know that television exposure grants them a kind of success, albeit
synthetic. For an instant they become heroes among their peers and
beyond. To be seen on television is somehow more real than life.

A few television reporters like Bill Moyers, who produced "The
Fire Next Door," the original CBS documentary that focused attention on the South Bronx, are sincerely troubled by shortcomings in
society, and are earnestly striving to place dealing with such situations higher on the national agenda. More generally, the media join
the policymakers to produce mirages to meet the public demand for
action, perhaps unaware they are doing so.

The image of David versus Goliath makes good media copy. The
New York Times, May 6, 1977, titled an article on 519 East 11th
Street, "State Tells Con Ed to Buy 2 Kilowatts—From a Windmill."
Another journalist, Allen Freeman, develops this image further in
"A Self-Help Housing Rehabilitation Effort Capped by Energy Con-
sciousness," which appeared in the February 1977 *AIA Journal*. Here
the quote, "A giant utility claims to be threatened by a lone urban

windmill," stands out in a text, accompanied by a photo, which admits:

> The symbolism of a free-spinning wind machine atop a low income tenement building has not been lost upon journalists and the opposition of Consolidated Edison has made a good story better. As chance would have it, a few blocks away from 519 (East 11th Street), by the East River, stands a Con Ed power plant with huge smokestacks.

The U-HAB Third Annual Progress Report reproduces the photo with the caption, "An outpost of rationality: windmill and solar panels on homesteading building (519 East 11th Street) are silhouetted against polluting Con Ed smokestacks."

For those still unsure how the system is beneficially being restructured by taxpayer investment in U-HAB, the August 1976 issue of *Supergirl* makes it clear. In one page it solves New York's intractable tangle of violent street gangs, heart-broken mothers, vandalism, and abandoned buildings. (See Figure 8–1). As The Hustlers ("the greatest street gang of them all") rebuild what the city condemned, a mysterious voice from the side points out, "And the city gave you professional help and supervision! Fabulous! "

A society that can place a man on the moon wants to believe that it can eradicate such mundane problems. The most skilled talents were deployed in the space race. In the South Bronx race, promise suffices. Complexity allows the media, the politicians, and the bureaucrats to fake it. Since actual success would be so difficult to attain in the South Bronx, these interests settle for solar windmills on tenant rehabilitated tenements, reasoning it is foolish to resist. For the politicians, reasoning with an expectant public can only result in replacement by another with bright promises; for the bureaucrats, reasoning can only develop focus on the red tape no one knows how to change. The rewards of appearing in the magic show instead are compelling, so the system takes the path of least resistance, thus warding off change.

WHAT IS THE HARM OF THIS MAGIC SHOW?

The defenders argue that the magic show sustains hope both on the part of the disadvantaged as well as of liberal citizens on their behalf. However, unfulfilled promises easily produce cynicism and alienation. Already there is much hidden damage.

Figure 8—1.   Supergirl

. . . Sweat Equity was even featured in Supergirl Comic Books . . .

SUPERGIRL is a trademark of DC Comics Inc. This illustration is © copyright 1973 DC Comics Inc. and is used with their permission.

Consider the following indictment delivered at the Fifth Annual Back to the City Conference, held in Hartford, Connecticut, October 1978. The president of Back to the City, Inc., Everett Ortner, remarked:

> The visitor to the modern American city asks his guide:
> "Who built that church?"
>   "H.H. Richardson."
> "Who built that building?"
>   "Louis Sullivan."
> "Who built that parking lot?"
>   "Urban Renewal."
> "Who created that garbage dump on a residential block?"
>   "Model Cities."

> Wherever I look in the American city I see the work of the federal tinkerer, reinforced by so much power that the movement of one of his fingers blots out a neighborhood, or slashes a scar through it for automobiles to ride on, or pushes down a historic public building, or any one of a hundred urban crimes.

> I have the very strong feeling that, beginning with FHA, forty-odd years ago, that if there had been no large-scale federal programs—no FHA, no HUD, no 236, no Section 8, no whatever—that New York City would be whole today, its magnificent housing stock still in use.

> I have asked others to comment on the possibility that many of our present urban ills are iatrogenic—the medical term for disease caused by the treatment itself of another ailment. Few care to say very much about it.

> I would like to say something about it. In my judgment, a very large proportion of our urban ailments is iatrogenic, caused by the ill-advised treatment by our specialists in urban affairs, Dr. Urban Renewal has been treating us all these years.

> When I say this to some people they reply—"Yes, but you can't change things now because there have been some failures. You'd just be throwing out the baby with the bath water."

> The truth is—I don't see many babies in the bath water. When I look down into it, I see staring back at me the faces of the politician, the bureaucrat, the professor of urbanology, the grants specialist, and the report writer. . . .

> The cities may yet be destroyed by people who play on your compassion for their own ends.

Here a voice is raised in warning, but most do not yet wish to heed it. Few believe HUD should be dismantled. Furthermore, removing any federal agency seems impossible as well as senseless until understanding of the basic problem improves.

Public interventions can be divided into three classes: beneficial, mixed, and harmful. The Housing Policy Law derived in Chapter 5, sustaining a predictable relationship between housing benefits and costs for all interests, can provide guidance in determining where each intervention belongs. In this light such public actions as zoning, consistent and systematic code enforcement, and equitable assistance to all eligible households are beneficial. Increasing complexity without compensatory overriding benefits is harmful in the long run. Public programs that raise false expectations, make promises that cannot be fulfilled, or establish an ever deepening dependence on assistance are in this latter class. Obviously it is important to be able to distinguish constructive interventions from harmful ones, but this is exactly what the magic show obscures. In contrast to reaching the moon, failures in distressed cities *can* be televised as successes.

Even as complexity masks what works, the magic show diverts attention and thereby action to the promising and innovative. Too often, the promising and innovative in fact do not work, but complexity permits enough doubts to persuade the participants themselves that they are effective and their promises are sincere.

Initiatives generally look beneficial to the average citizen and there are no recognized experts to prevent unproductive efforts. Who then wants to be an ordinary code inspector telling people they must make repairs when the kudos go to those who bring lower interest mortgage money? But consider 3 percent Home Improvement Loans, called Section 312. One might expect these to induce renovations by homeowners who feel they cannot afford a bank loan for this purpose.

Section 312 is frequently counterproductive in stimulating renovation in at least three ways: it can cause postponement of repairs, discourage homeostasis, and promote more rapid gentrification and displacement. The problems begin when there is—not in appearance but in fact—too little to go around, which is virtually always the case. Once homeowners have heard about 3 percent loans many decide to wait their turn rather than borrow at conventional rates over 12 percent. Thus, they are induced to procrastinate in renovation, instead of taking that stitch in time.

Sometimes the assistance goes to disadvantaged households, often not regarded locally as more deserving. Families with savings do not see why others on similar incomes without savings should get priority. If minority families are helped affirmatively, jealousies become only sharper, as local norms of fair play are violated. It may be a national goal to reduce discrimination, but here prejudices are not changed but reinforced. The stronger community members either begin to carp about the situation or quietly leave.

On other occasions, the limited 3 percent assistance may spur gentrification as assistance is granted to those better able to comply with the paperwork, those with clear title to their property, or those who are most active in refurbishing the neighborhood. Here again it seems virtually impossible for outside bureaucracies to consistently tilt the benefits toward the disadvantaged. Rather, such programs tend to fragment or polarize communities. Media stories, however, usually focus on the positive aspects, allowing Section 312 to continue in its present form, doing more harm than good.

This example, showing how a limited pool of Section 312 assistance often turns out to be harmful while being shown as helpful, is representative of too many forms of federal intervention to be ignored. Because of complexity, definitive evaluations of such programs are impossible. That debate can never be resolved as long as strong special interests, often with the best intentions, can secure favorable media coverage. Thus the show goes on while cynicism grows. Because of complexity, the disadvantaged end up with more promises than lasting benefits.

The solution lies in realizing that many governmental programs only appear to be neutral tools for revitalizing neighborhoods. Under cover of favorable publicity that plays on naive assumptions, the self-interests of bureaucracies, politicians, and neighborhood leaders bootstrapping themselves all skillfully fight for survival.

DO NEIGHBORHOOD INITIATIVES HOLD ANY PROMISE?

The actual initiatives are often instructive examples of community autonomy and intelligent applications of the available federal tools. It is important to understand how they become coopted and how self-reliance is sometimes preserved in spite of a debilitating system that reacts to ward off change with extraordinary cunning.

The magic show masks a fundamental and dynamic tension between neighborhood leadership and dependence. The media appeal of the initiatives lies in their autonomy as they display local intelligence in selectively heeding sensible laws, ignoring others, and fashioning missing elements from the resources at hand. The dominant system responds covertly. Instinctively threatened, it strives to reestablish dependence upon it, trying to coopt these local initiatives at every turn.

As described in the South Bronx above, public officials are often put under the gun to do something, both to show results and to pursue ancillary goals such as minority hiring or integration. This becomes easier when they take control, distorting the original successful neighborhood initiative. However, a serious, consistent distortion generally enters in the replicating process. When policy-makers begin pushing any program for action rather than responding to a natural pull from the initiators, polarization becomes more likely than community building. Instead of strictly holding to a responsive posture, the agency becomes action-oriented, a critical difference. Instead of the community being in the driver's seat, the agency takes command, and the community fragments into separate passengers not agreed on a common destination, but instead commonly critical of the driver. If the vehicle now goes anywhere, it is in spite of the community.

This tension between autonomy and dependence seems to pervade many federal interventions in neighborhoods from Model Cities to Community Development Block Grants (CDBG) and possibly explains much of the growing national sense of frustration with national urban policies.

The Neighborhood Housing Services (NHS) efforts stand out as a contrasting model that encourages local autonomy in expansion and survives replication. Wherever NHS is successful, control is truly shared, something immediately apparent regardless of who shows off the local NHS—the banker, city official, or resident. Here each role and responsibility is defined mutually by a partnership of community forces, lenders from the private sector, and public officials. Instead of bankers red-lining a neighborhood because loan risks appear too great while politicians and bureaucrats pursue their roles in the magic show, here public monies are focused on eliminating these risks while residents direct municipal code enforcement. Then banks can loan and residents can regain confidence to fix up their own homes conventionally.

NHS establishes a consensus among all the affected interests on what is fair as it goes along. This critical difference is something the producers of the magic show cannot generally allow. The Urban Reinvestment Task Force (URTF), which has fostered the replication of NHS in many cities, has had to fight off absorption of this new type of revitalization initiative by HUD—another clue to the federal co-opting tendencies.

The sage above who saw no baby in the bathwater could easily believe that HUD is under some compulsion to coopt any promising initiative. HUD's survival seems to depend increasingly on sleight of hand. Critics have become less important than what the media broadcast. HUD may even be using increasingly scarce assistance to produce next year's program: X dollars ear-marked for another promising development by Spanish-speaking minorities, Y amount for congregate elderly accommodations in an abandoned school, Z effort for innovations preventing displacement in a gentrifying neighborhood, and so forth. The Section 8 housing assistance is already prespecified for the ablest developers in each of these categories and the bureaucrats stand by to cut the red tape confronting these demonstration initiatives so they will be on hand for media broadcast on schedule. Otherwise HUD fears the public would discover the lack of a coherent urban policy and begin asking probing questions, threatening the federal bureaucracies.

WHAT CAN BE DONE ABOUT THE MAGIC SHOW?

Clearly whoever succeeds in designing a better mousetrap will quickly encounter the producers of the magic show to buy in, share the credit, and broadcast the news of his new device. If he sells out too cheaply or is coopted, then the public has simply been fooled once again. Unless one can ensure that neighborhood self-interests remain paramount, the implied promise of the initiative will likely prove false.

The federal tool chest of assistance is often utilized in creative ways by innovative local initiatives because these neighborhood groups have a sense of where they are going and can fashion missing elements. However, the tool chest not only comes with out-of-date or misleading instructions that discourage fresh applications but also with bureaucrats under pressure to bend the tools to their own ends. The bureaucrats do not see the overall picture but rather have the next magic show in mind and will unconsciously coopt if necessary to meet their schedule. This will thwart neighborhood self-reliance in the long run. A dependence on both HUD and the local bureaucracy is thereby fostered and then maintained through lowered neighborhood confidence and reduced autonomy. This may preserve the bureaucracies and even reelect politicians but it is not in the long-run public interest.

When confronted by urgent urban needs and obviously inadequate means, the rational response is either to scale down the expectations or find ways to leverage resources more effectively. The complex system that allows the urban predicament to persist has instead found ways to mask the obvious inadequacy with media success stories and earnest posturing. The voters and taxpayers have charged their government with responsibilities they neither understood nor wish to shoulder. They are to blame if under these impossible pressures their politicians and bureaucrats discover that the magic show offers them a way to survive. Scale down the expectations or find the resources and the magic show will no longer be necessary.

Chapter 9

Improving Local Government Response to Neighborhood Dynamics

Many policymakers at all levels of government appear to have lost sight of what works and have instead become absorbed in more dramatic actions whose outcome might be more harmful than good. How did this come about? How can the babel of divergent expectations be tempered? What realities must be accepted by the many interests tangled in the urban predicament before matters can improve?

DRAWING INFERENCES FROM A MEDICAL METAPHOR

A medical analogy can guide the search for public initiatives that build neighborhood confidence. A patient seeks a doctor when he feels ill. The doctor attempts to determine what is wrong and to learn what will enable the patient's system to return to normal. He often suggests the proverbial chicken soup and bedrest because the human system is homeostatic and remarkably self-correcting. However, doctors sometimes become so involved in treating the disease rather than the patients that others come to prescribe secondary medication to counteract the side effects of the primary drugs prescribed to restore the patient's health. Cases of iatrogenic, or doctor-induced, illness are becoming common and result in dependence on medicine. A movement is building to work more closely with nature and to restore medicine to the care of a practitioner who deals with the whole patient and directs the specialists.

Similarly, planning must redefine urban health and the planners' supportive responsibilities. Neighborhoods are also living ecosystems, complete with many unrecognized self-healing properties. Just as fever or allergic reactions signal very different imbalances in the organic system, lack of maintenance or speculation indicate quite different imbalances in specific neighborhoods. Yet now, when there is urban distress, what prescriptions can planners offer? Do they even try to diagnose what ails the particular neighborhood? Are there any equivalents to temperature and pulse rate?

Planners do not attempt to diagnose different neighborhood imbalances systematically. They simply offer broad spectrum federal programs, unaware that the programs are sometimes helpful, but more often harmful. These remedies sound like alphabet soup: FACE, 312, UDAG, NSA, FNMA, NHS, and the like.* No one has ever seriously considered the secondary effects. It is unclear how the specialists expect neighborhoods to actually improve. As a result, revitalization is an unanticipated surprise to many.

In remote areas of the third world, Western visitors are often approached by people begging for medicine. No doctor would condone giving away drugs, yet such a visitor probably knows more about what his medicine might do to the beggar than is known about the ultimate impact of granting an Urban Development Action Grant (UDAG) to a financially distressed urban area. Are planners trying to obtain and administer one-shot, pump-priming assistance that restores self-reliance, or make whole cities dependent on long-term life-support systems?

INSIGHTS GAINED FROM WORKSHOPS EXPLORING NEIGHBORHOOD DYNAMICS

SRI International at Stanford, with National Science Foundation funding, reviewed a promising array of governance tools employed in thirty cities for neighborhood revitalization, including performance incentives, taxation and regulatory devices, stimulation of the private sector, and institutional reforms (SRI, 1979). SRI found that this was like discovering a pharmacy with some new medicines without having a doctor or an accepted medical theory. To overcome this, to match these new tools to their appropriate neighborhood context, a small group developed a simulation game called Jarvis, U.S.A.,

---

*Federally assisted code enforcement (FACE); Section 312 low interest loans; Urban Development Action Grants (UDAG); Neighborhood Strategies Areas (NSA); Federal National Mortgage Association (FNMA); and Neighborhood Housing Services (NHS).

more highly educated newcomers. Each participant chose a team role which he did *not* play in real life, but with which he had contended. The mayor was provided with a hidden agenda of challenges and changes in assistance programs to be introduced during the game.

Each team initially framed its objectives for the neighborhood, defining how it would wish to see Gastown transformed in the coming years, but was restricted to six simple tools for intervention:

- Any conceivable green-lining bank commitment
- Any neighborhood marketing effort
- Obtaining historic district designation
- 50 Section 8 rental assistance commitments
- 100 Section 312 rehabilitation commitments
- $600,000 in Community Development Block Grants (for any eligible use like street repairs, patrolpersons' benefits, housing fixup incentives, etc.)

The participants relished caricaturing their opposites, but soon realized the power of City Hall in controlling all federal tools. While the preservationists were easily able to integrate their objectives with the CDBG planner's agenda, the two advocate roles were much more difficult to define.

This game suggested that the dictates of economics and privilege translate more easily into local practice than the rights of the disadvantaged, whether poor or black. The ethics of earn and deserve all too easily dominate the rights of those already there if the latter are unable to assert themselves legally or politically. This situation seems unlikely to change unless the neighborhood and black advocates can find common cause with or out-maneuvering the establishment and more privileged interests.

If one can generalize from this simulation, then the disadvantaged would gain more by working within the dominant earn/deserve ethic than by appealing rhetorically on the basis of special needs and prior rights. Federal assistance programs for the Have-Nots mislead dangerously when their promises prove unattainable. Such needs and rights are likely to remain a frustrating illusion for the disadvantaged unless they become more fully accepted by the dominant majority of society. Now things seem to be going the other way.

A number of further insights emerged:

- If no consensus plan acceptable to all interests develops, confusion or irrelevant actions take over. The media exacerbate these around the neighborhood classification matrix presented in Chapter 3 (SRI, 1978).

Most participants, themselves planners, found the dynamics in the Jarvis neighborhoods easy to differentiate. All concurred in their descriptions. Two important discoveries emerged. First, they admitted that in their own cities they would be reluctant to differentiate neighborhoods publicly for fear of self-fulfilling responses and resident antagonism. Unlike doctors, they preferred to withhold their diagnoses. Without any planning theory to back them up, this is understandable.

The second discovery was more startling: prescriptions varied widely. Playing Jarvis allows sharp differences in ideology to emerge which are normally hidden by the complexity of the real urban scene. Some wanted to save the housing by excluding what they saw as forces of decline, while others sought to aid the disadvantaged. None wanted to reduce government intervention—most wanted to prescribe as much and as many different programs as possible. The Jeffersonian idea that the government that governs least governs best seemed alien to these planners. Scarcely any added up the incurred costs. Many players felt called upon to do something, acting as if they were encouraging maximum participation to a free smorgasbord.

While this simulation was only a game, it suggested that, for lack of any accepted theory of urban health and supporting indicators, practicing planners are covertly pursuing remedial tactics that are based on conflicting ideologies. They not only see little to be gained by differentiating neighborhoods on the basis of their dynamics, but seldom have a coherent rationale in mind while intervening. Furthermore, it suggests that individually they are rarely equipped to face or deal with the ambiguities and conflicts accompanying change that will dissipate or absorb most of their energies.

A different simulation was designed to explore the conflicting ideologies encountered in gentrifying neighborhoods (City Living, 1978). Its purpose was to sharpen participant awareness of the various agendas and to discover how more of the benefits of revitalization could flow to existing residents. Here the emphasis was placed on team interactions among four ideological caricatures: *CDBG planner, ethnic advocate, black advocate,* and *historic preservationist.* (Table 2—2 was developed for this workshop.)

The materials presented to the participants described a gentrifying neighborhood called Gastown, composed of decent, working-class, and prestige housing near the city center, shared in 1970 by elderly East European ethnics and minorities, but recently attracting young,

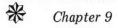 *Chapter 9*

Improving Local Government Response to Neighborhood Dynamics

Many policymakers at all levels of government appear to have lost sight of what works and have instead become absorbed in more dramatic actions whose outcome might be more harmful than good. How did this come about? How can the babel of divergent expectations be tempered? What realities must be accepted by the many interests tangled in the urban predicament before matters can improve?

DRAWING INFERENCES FROM A MEDICAL METAPHOR

A medical analogy can guide the search for public initiatives that build neighborhood confidence. A patient seeks a doctor when he feels ill. The doctor attempts to determine what is wrong and to learn what will enable the patient's system to return to normal. He often suggests the proverbial chicken soup and bedrest because the human system is homeostatic and remarkably self-correcting. However, doctors sometimes become so involved in treating the disease rather than the patients that others come to prescribe secondary medication to counteract the side effects of the primary drugs prescribed to restore the patient's health. Cases of iatrogenic, or doctor-induced, illness are becoming common and result in dependence on medicine. A movement is building to work more closely with nature and to restore medicine to the care of a practitioner who deals with the whole patient and directs the specialists.

Similarly, planning must redefine urban health and the planners' supportive responsibilities. Neighborhoods are also living ecosystems, complete with many unrecognized self-healing properties. Just as fever or allergic reactions signal very different imbalances in the organic system, lack of maintenance or speculation indicate quite different imbalances in specific neighborhoods. Yet now, when there is urban distress, what prescriptions can planners offer? Do they even try to diagnose what ails the particular neighborhood? Are there any equivalents to temperature and pulse rate?

Planners do not attempt to diagnose different neighborhood imbalances systematically. They simply offer broad spectrum federal programs, unaware that the programs are sometimes helpful, but more often harmful. These remedies sound like alphabet soup: FACE, 312, UDAG, NSA, FNMA, NHS, and the like.* No one has ever seriously considered the secondary effects. It is unclear how the specialists expect neighborhoods to actually improve. As a result, revitalization is an unanticipated surprise to many.

In remote areas of the third world, Western visitors are often approached by people begging for medicine. No doctor would condone giving away drugs, yet such a visitor probably knows more about what his medicine might do to the beggar than is known about the ultimate impact of granting an Urban Development Action Grant (UDAG) to a financially distressed urban area. Are planners trying to obtain and administer one-shot, pump-priming assistance that restores self-reliance, or make whole cities dependent on long-term life-support systems?

INSIGHTS GAINED FROM WORKSHOPS
EXPLORING NEIGHBORHOOD DYNAMICS

SRI International at Stanford, with National Science Foundation funding, reviewed a promising array of governance tools employed in thirty cities for neighborhood revitalization, including performance incentives, taxation and regulatory devices, stimulation of the private sector, and institutional reforms (SRI, 1979). SRI found that this was like discovering a pharmacy with some new medicines without having a doctor or an accepted medical theory. To overcome this, to match these new tools to their appropriate neighborhood context, a small group developed a simulation game called Jarvis, U.S.A.,

---

*Federally assisted code enforcement (FACE); Section 312 low interest loans; Urban Development Action Grants (UDAG); Neighborhood Strategies Areas (NSA); Federal National Mortgage Association (FNMA); and Neighborhood Housing Services (NHS).

tendencies by focusing on these side shows, which the public confuses with the norm.

- Unilateral progress by any interest toward its objectives was difficult, especially for the advocates of the disadvantaged. However,
each could easily thwart the progress of the others.

- Once mistrust is present in the system, any plan or written docu-
ment can more easily polarize the situation because it serves as
grist for the conflicting interests. To avoid opposition, care must
be taken to gain the support of all interests to any intervention
that cannot be imposed.

Such workshops shed light on the nature of the urban predicament. Without a comprehensive theory of urban dynamics that considers divergent expectations, ideological tangles are likely to grow as
each interest attempts to fortify its stand. The confusion only benefits those who can still discern and pursue their self-interests—the
more sophisticated and the unscrupulous.

THREE CITY EXAMPLES

The real world is not as clear cut as simulations. Some lessons can be
drawn from the rich variety of different city styles. Illustrations are
useful.

Baltimore is considered a model by many independent professional planners because it demonstrates a successful application of
federal resources to neighborhood demands.

Years ago Baltimore developed a housing court—it now has a
service-oriented code enforcement administration that offers technical assistance along with sanctions. It was early in anticipating the
extent of the red-lining problem, and now has an elaborate system of
homeownership loans supported by bond issues and federal funding.

Neighborhood Housing Services has already evolved in Baltimore
beyond the initial Pittsburgh model and is now creatively marketing
local housing opportunities, both to residents and to newcomers.

Some years ago the public servants in Baltimore were considered
aloof, but neighborhood groups, after gaining strength in organizing
against them, now find the well-coordinated city agency unusually
responsive in housing and development matters. The officials appear
courteous, professional, and considerate of neighborhood views.
Moreover, they only embark on new programs in response to neighborhood initiatives. Officials and community interests treat each

other respectfully as peers, not with mistrust or paternal condescension. Citizens feel the professionalism and competence of the public sector saved Baltimore from becoming another Newark—that is, the media image of Newark.

New York seems to undertake actions only *in extremis*, when pushes and shoves by tenacious special interests and the media render simply standing still no longer possible. Special projects are continually being advanced by the New York planners, which seem Rube Goldberg devices of elaborate intricacy. Minority corporations favored by special assistance have managed to redo a score of large multifamily structures among the uncounted thousands abandoned by rational investors because of New York's confusing web of laws, administrative regulations, and red tape.

As federal support is brought in by the planners, solar gardens and windmill generators sprout on rooftops and are heralded by the media as promising initiatives, confusing the public by encouraging expectations to soar, while the tangle of impediments confronting neighborhood project initiators becomes ever more staggering. Higher level officials, seeking "replicable initiatives," obtain special exceptions for these demonstrations, but are finding their facilitating role growing to a full time occupation. These officials are unable to curb the generally arrogant and obstinate bureaucracy which cannot deliver what people want.

Other resident groups, trying to undertake similar ventures, find themselves stumped by an administration that appears hostile or surly to them, incompetent, and dominated by over-age party hacks. Rage and frustration are not far below the surface.

Boston is a maverick. It has devised some innovative housing improvement programs that minimize red tape and allow owners to do as much renovation as they care to themselves in response to direct cash rebates. It is also creatively marketing its weaker housing, diffusing gentrification, and minimizing displacement. This indirectly induces much renovation without raising expectations or the need for lower interest municipal loan funds. This patina of innovation masks serious fiscal strains, property tax problems, and other basic municipal shortcomings, including an aura of corruption maintained by media investigations.

Boston's administrative structure appears complex and ever-changing. It mixes older bureaucrats with young, inexperienced, and fresh faces, without continuity. Promising neighborhood initiatives tend to become co-opted by the public sector rather than develop into partnership ventures. Although overall housing demand balances supply, these uncertainties keep city residents uneasy about the future, thereby holding back major investment.

THE BUREAUCRATIC RESPONSE
TO COMPLEXITY

It is useful to focus on how the system now responds to excessive complexity in such cities. Unless bureaucracies have clear goals, they easily get into disarray and increase the confusion.

In Baltimore, public effort is more productive because comparatively little energy is dissipated in deadlocks. This exemplifies a valuable synergism. In such settings the team members know each other's roles, strengths, and weaknesses. Jurisdictions are clearer and ambiguities are not left unresolved. Citizens are less likely to play one public actor against another. Trust develops among team members, and in this supportive climate creative and innovative partnerships begin to develop. No longer does each interest concentrate on playing it safe.

When the public actors are confident in what they are doing and see themselves as members of a well-coordinated team, the special competencies and initiatives of each member are supported. *The focus is on what actually works rather than on what looks promising.* In practice this is becoming comparatively rare. More frequently, ambiguity concerning program purpose results in preoccupation with job security. This cripples the responsiveness of many urban bureaucracies, as each employee defends his position saying in effect: "I only work here, but I'm doing my job as they've defined it!"

Overly complex and rapidly changing organizational structure allows bureaucrats to behave in ways that reflect little respect for the public, their actual employers. When job tenure is too secure, letters go unanswered, phone calls are left on hold, and arrogance sets in. Firing someone for surliness or incompetence is a start, if it can be done and peers agree it is deserved. But seeking refuge in job security and perennial reorganizations are really signs that the public sector has failed to properly define program purpose.

Other signs of disarray are tangled municipal responsibilities, passing the buck, rising rates of straw ownership, and arson for profit. When these are present, public resources are likely to be consumed in counterproductive conflict.

In overly complex administrations a vicious cycle develops. Goal ambiguities are left unresolved as expectations become less and less attainable. Two trends in the staffing of higher, policymaking positions are symptoms of this deteriorating situation. First, the ambitious replace the seasoned actors. The only visible warning is when wiser professionals begin to decline positions as untenable regardless of compensation because they sense the task, as currently defined, cannot be successfully completed. Into this vacuum step younger, more ambitious individuals eager to gain experience, status, and recognition, but with little to lose. The basic need to rationalize the structure of the public sector is further masked as tenderfoots learn the ropes in policy jobs involving citizens' welfare. Paradoxically this allows the system to grow even more complex and counterintuitive. It then becomes even easier to hide the lack of substantive results. Soon one can no longer differentiate beneficial from harmful public programs.

Second, excessive complexity allows fuzzy thinking to pervade the entire system, until all are equally unaware of inherent goal ambiguities and are thus powerless to resolve them. Individuals promoted to leadership roles appear unperturbed by goal conflicts or rhetorically accept them as political challenges. These leaders seem articulate, but their words actually have little meaning. Further, their actions appear inconsistent with their words—and contradictory impressions emerge of where they actually stand on issues.

Unresolved complexity now permits many public administrations at all levels—from the federal bureaucracies to city halls—to avoid the task of rigorously defining everyone's role and responsibilities. *Abetted by superficial media coverage, which can make the novel seem promising, policymakers pursue dramatically innovative instead of mundane efforts that actually work. This only widens the gap between expectations and reality.*

Has society become so gullible and so hurried that the need to think things through is no longer recognized? That is the impression one gets from many cities. Fortunately there are important differences in approach between cities, suggesting that ways to overcome the problems of excessive complexity and uncertainty can still be found.

HOW THE URBAN SYSTEM HAS ALTERED

The urban predicament seems to have become one of man's most counterintuitive creations. Its complexity virtually defies analysis from within. It seems the convolutions of the system now exceed our ability to obtain, transmit, retrieve, and utilize current and reliable information. Fundamental changes occur largely undetected. A number of basic changes are intertwined:

- Responsibility and accountability at the neighborhood level are diminished;
- Expectations of what is possible have soared;
- Decisions made elsewhere are difficult to alter and have unintended and unrecognized local consequences;
- Responsibility for the disadvantaged has been relinquished to the federal government and federal assistance fragments communities;
- Citizens have come to mistake media images of the new or sensational for the norm.

Finding the causal links among these changes seems impossible, but their implications cannot be ignored.

There were serious inequities in the past and people sometimes felt helpless, but they were forced to be realistic in dealing with actions threatening their homes and neighborhood. As any community experienced in or out migrations, calamities, and boom or bust, its churches, businesses, and charities did what they could to ease the lot of the disadvantaged. Forces shaped behavior to counter unbalancing influences. In living systems this is called homeostasis.

Now, local feedback is no longer effective in shaping behavior and expectations. For example, a home buyer used to obtain funds that were neighbors' deposits granted as a mortgage from the local bank. Then the secondary mortgage market was created to improve liquidity. Now a larger, computerized downtown bank issues the mortgage, insures it with outsiders, and resells it on the national secondary market, retaining only the servicing function. This bank is stripped of the many ancillary roles the old-fashioned banker played and accepts the way national insurers and mortgage purchasers downgrade urban loans. At the same time more people have come to view a mortgage as an American right. This leads to awareness of red-lining. Since local forces can no longer fine-tune neighborhood dynamics, homeostasis has been undermined. In the long run, these little unnoticed sacrifices in local responsibility can destabilize the whole system.

The people's expectations of government, of what it can and should do, have been so dramatically altered that inherent contradictions are no longer recognized. Among its conflicting roles are: employer of the unemployed, balance wheel of the economy, lender for special needs, and houser of last resort. An especially difficult new role is advocate of the disadvantaged.

President Eisenhower's suggestion that everyone should have at least a median income is unattainable of course, but federal policy has been groping toward this objective for some time. In the past, community influentials determined the redistribution to help the poor. Even if judgments were harsh, there was no recourse.

Today, it is increasingly difficult to determine how best to help the disadvantaged. More and more people feel qualified for aid. Entire cities feel needy. Should they still try to be self-reliant, seeking only a minimum of outside pump-priming assistance to get back on course? Why not tackle ambitious urban reconstruction programs expecting Washington to underwrite their massive costs?

Most communities now receive sharply increased federal assistance in a bewildering array of programs to help their poor and others in hard times. However, this array of programs fashioned in Washington has many unintended consequences. The accompanying increase in bureaucracy has invisibly eroded community self-reliance. More laws, regulations, and new attitudes have made the local banker, the real estate broker, the neighborhood school, and the local tax assessor simple cogs in a system grown so complex its linkages can no longer be discerned.

Initially this loss of community is neither apparent to influentials nor visible in hard indicators, but when the Federal Housing Authority began to promote homeownership with low down payment urban mortgages (under Section 203b and 235), conventional lenders yielded to unregulated mortgage brokers. In Detroit, Chicago, and St. Louis whole neighborhoods became crippled by abandonment as some absentee owners made their welfare tenants into homeowners at substantial profit to themselves and some middlemen (Downie 1974, Boyer 1973). More recently, under Fair Access to Insurance Requirements (FAIR) Plan insurance, arson for profit has developed into a similar urban pathology.

Remote bureaucracies react too sluggishly and then miss the point that local responsibility and accountability are vital and must be encouraged. The debate on causes of urban distress continues unresolved while each specialized bureaucracy requires even more paperwork to protect itself. Increasingly complex and everchanging programs are tried, obscuring the situation hopelessly.

Not only are remote decisions unlikely to suit all local situations, but they are extremely difficult to influence or alter. Just as the pace of change accelerates, the lag time for bureaucratic turn around increases. When outsiders with inadequate means to meet expectations short circuit the local system, unintended consequences result. Simply adding local input to the national policymaking process is no answer. That only compounds the situation. As long as complex programs are designed and regulated from Washington, neighborhoods will be vulnerable to exploitation whenever remote decisions are locally inappropriate.

In the area of civil rights, federal presence has helped bring about a local rethinking of minority rights; but whenever promises raise expectations beyond the attainable, the poor bear the brunt. Even as local policymakers struggle to deal with the inherent contradictions among the government's roles, the federal government offers block grants. This discretionary money does not require defense at the voting booth like property taxes or bond issues. It looks deceptively free, but along with it come separate local counter bureaucracies for each program to see that the spending complies with the ill-defined national agenda. General revenue sharing, the Community Employment and Training Assistance (CETA) program, and Community Development Block Grants (CDBG) are only the most visible examples. Instead of developing communities, such aid often undermines and fragments them when splinter groups try to get from Washington what they cannot obtain locally.

Many local participants accept the usefulness of federal programs and evaluations on faith, but are themselves preoccupied with making them work. Everyone seems to lack an overview, and the public sector's response to all societal shortcomings has become addressing the symptom rather than the source. The result is a worsening of the symptoms while the root causes remain untouched. In describing similar problems, Wendell Berry has said:

> . . . we have to see again, as the founders of our government saw, that the most appropriate governmental powers are negative—those, that is, that protect the small and the weak from the great and the powerful, not those by which the government becomes the profligate and ineffectual parent of the small and the weak after it has permitted the great and powerful to make them helpless. (Berry, 1977: 219).

In some urban neighborhoods conventional market functions such as development, construction, management, investment, and insurance are becoming distorted or have ceased. As the public sector intervenes, the situation often deteriorates further. Here:

- Public sector responsibility for identifying the problems is confused with responsibility for developing a solution;

- Lack of understanding by virtually all concerned of how the market functions makes it difficult to achieve agreement on the nature of the problem and the appropriateness of particular remedies;

- The private sector has come to mistrust the public sector and any remedies proposed by it;

- The public sector no longer knows how to work with the private sector and mistrusts private sector interests;

- Mechanisms that can mediate the differences are few and unrecognized, while communication between interests deteriorates and polarization increases; and

- The unscrupulous discover how they can exploit the situation.

Ways out of this predicament are not at all clear but measures that improve confidence, clarity, competence, and open communication are moves in the right direction. Such measures restore the function of the market. *Because markets handle much more complex tasks than individuals can ever understand, interventions to deal with market imperfections and to achieve social goals should work indirectly through the market, not directly short circuit it, whenever possible.*

More regulation, in spite of best intentions, often turns out to be self-defeating. Instead, *more of the workings of the system must be opened to public scrutiny so that alert citizens can pressure for vital change.*

The most promising basic alterations that meet the above criteria are more disclosure coupled with the phasing out of obsolete government functions, or **sunshine** *and* **sunset** *laws.*

WHAT CAN NOW BE DONE?

Describing the problems has been much simpler than prescribing solutions. However some possible courses of action suggest themselves.

Policymakers urgently need a better understanding of the overall picture than they now have. What are the current demand and supply dynamics in each region, city, and neighborhood? Mismatches here exert profound but unrecognized influences on all local expectations and behavior. Prerequisites for improving the urban predicament are to build a better information base out of time series data as discussed in Chapter 3, and to increase general understanding about contextual variables through indirect research approaches, as described in Chapter 4. These are appropriately done by federal agencies.

What are the expectations of each and every interest? These are best mapped locally. Policymakers must plan and act in partnership with all the affected interests in ways that constantly relate expectations to reality. The Mayor's Advisory Council (MAC) in Denver is a promising example of rebuilding a participatory neighborhood development process. Open evening forums at City Hall, patiently chaired by a local banker and attended by concerned residents, councilmen, and public officials are slowly rebuilding trust between participants that had seriously eroded.

Margaret Mead pointed out in another context that a people can report how the shoe pinches, but experts must either figure out how to ease the pinches or they must help the people accept them. By this test, urban policymakers fail if they simply deliver federal palliatives to stabilize neighborhood dynamics, even if that seems to be what the people expect.

The Housing Policy Law developed in Chapter 5 can guide policymakers: the long-term housing benefits and costs attached to any public intervention must remain predictable and seem fair to every interest. This will force planners to abandon their time-worn practice of direct intervention based on obsolete assumptions. If inequities felt in the system are not adequately addressed, then society will ultimately revoke the trust and power delegated to its policymakers.

Policymakers now face a number of critical distractions, each of which is probably more harmful than helpful: administering unworkable, complex assistance programs, dealing with media impact when it diverts efforts from what works and disguises what does not, building sophisticated data systems that only impress the uninitiated, and getting bogged down in the vast swamps of ideological debates.

Better indicators of urban disarray could help avert the distractions. The government as public servant seems to be the logical agent because better indicators must be developed by some entity with an interest in the continuing viability of urban areas. Yet can it do the job? The public sector is in a state of confusion in many cities. As the national media featured Cleveland's bankruptcy, other cities reassured themselves by asserting that "it couldn't happen here." However, danger signs are up in many larger cities. Increasing ambiguity in urban property values, more straw ownership and dubious financing, arson, and the courts attempts to resolve public issues— these are all signs of urban vitality hemorrhaging. Some cities can afford more population or capital flight than others before they become fiscally anemic.

Timely resolution might be aided if independent agents, like those who rate municipal bonds, developed comparative indices of urban health such as declining private investment in development, excessive volatility of local housing markets, rising incidence of straw ownership, or fires of suspicious origin per 1,000 dwelling units. Just having such yardsticks would exert a beneficial influence, although it is unclear how such indicators can be made operational. Perhaps an urban Sierra Club or Common Cause could take on the development of such indicators.

If bond ratings reflected such factors, or federal assistance were withheld on this basis, municipal attention might be re-directed to deal with the determinants of urban health instead of being devoted to federal grantsmanship and maintaining high bond ratings. This would radically modify the basis for obtaining federal assistance to include measuring the capacity to use it effectively.

The recent federal history of aiding special interests, developers, and political constituencies in distressed cities, coupled with the sheer size and inertia of not only the Washington bureaucracies but also their locally spawned counterparts, suggests that producing such a turnaround will prove arduous. Special interests will constrain the turnaround from every side. But continuing on the present course will ultimately prove much more hazardous and costly, even if currently the danger signs are still masked.

In regions where overall demand is slack, appropriate policy choices differ radically from the alternatives open to areas with surging demand. Until these historically unprecedented tides are recognized, and policies are differentiated accordingly, both national and local neighborhood policy debates will remain frustrating and futile. Policymakers must develop a sound basis for knowing when, where, and how to intervene to stabilize dynamics so that they ease the pinches. Chapters 3 and 4 (especially Figures 3–1, 3–3, and 4–1) serve only to scout this new terrain.

HOW CAN DESIRABLE CHANGE COME ABOUT?

Fresh opportunities for synergetic neighborhood programs present themselves in all cities from time to time, but only in some situations do they develop into a self-sustaining approach. Like engines being cranked, many cities show promising starts, but comparatively few are developing any real momentum.

Consider lending once more as an illustration. Some time ago public, private, and community interests lost sight of the many aspects of mortgage credit and the roles bankers formerly played in maintaining neighborhoods. Without this basic understanding, national secondary mortgage market criteria, grading old home mortgages at a lower rating than new home loans, were not directly challenged. Instead, people organized to battle against a symptom: red-lining.

Recently, however, the Philadelphia Mortgage Plan evolved as a creative, locally tailored answer to such mortgage problems after a thorough local re-examination of far more than just lending criteria. Before this plan emerged, combining a large urban mortgage pool with a review process for marginal applications, the roles and responsibilities of every public and private actor were redefined in a painstaking process. This has become easy to avoid, but citizens and planners must undertake some such searching process of defining their common goals before a promising revitalization model can be developed. Indeed, Pittsburgh underwent similar experiences before Neighborhood Housing Services first evolved, and now the Urban Reinvestment Task Force makes such a process a precondition before it will assist in developing a Neighborhood Housing Services program in any city.

Initiating a Neighborhood Housing Services Program is one of the most promising vehicles for instilling the appropriate and responsive attitudes among public, private, and community interests because it helps clarify roles and tempers expectations with reality. Revitalizing a neighborhood requires bringing private, public, and community interests into sensitive partnerships so its problems are seen as common problems. As urban interests diverge into adversarial roles, this allows confusion and mistrust to rise. Here neighborhood deterioration becomes as much a matter of confidence as of available resident incomes. Genuine partnerships must be forged from the diverging interests to revitalize the spirit of the neighborhood residents into improving their homes, and Neighborhood Housing Services has become one of the most promising vehicles for this.

To illustrate: a Boston housing inspector was transformed when he became assigned to Neighborhood Housing Services. He began to appreciate the reasons for coding dwellings, realized he was tied into a coherent team effort to fix up a neighborhood, and started to volunteer constructive ideas. Likewise a Boston bank president, who had earlier participated in a court suit to enjoin mortgage disclosure, helped create a mortgage review board, hired community staff, and developed a green-lining program as he discovered what he could do as an urban lender.

It is too soon to tell whether the presence of the Neighborhood Housing Services vehicle in Boston is anything more than a promising sputter in mitigating distrust and transforming bureaucracy. Baltimore, on the other hand, with a showcase Neighborhood Housing

Service currently appears to be humming. However, developing synergism is much more complex than simply reorganizing to be like Baltimore.

Baltimore's Housing and Community Development Agency has gathered all the municipal functions that affect neighborhoods into one executive super agency. This may be helpful in improving top-down communication and coordination, but it does not assure sensitivity to changing neighborhood dynamics. Baltimore's administration currently seems to be a well-coordinated bureaucracy, smoothly delivering programs. However, it may be slower than one with some creative discord to discover and creatively respond to changed circumstances. Perhaps no coordinated bureaucracy can rapidly redirect itself without being jarred by a major offensive. As yet, then, there is no one clear model to follow.

Increased understanding of which interest seeks what, when, and where can help policymakers understand the urban dynamics. Workshops, role playing exercises, and simulations like those mentioned earlier in this chapter can help reveal important aspects of the complex urban system. They are the closest thing to a laboratory that planners can devise. Obviously coming up with an effective national policy context that respects neighborhood integrity still lies ahead. There is not much that can be done locally without a change in national approach.

CONCLUSION: SOME MORE IMMEDIATE STEPS

As the pace of change quickens and some neighborhoods unexpectedly revitalize, urban policymakers will need more responsive indicators for detecting change. Classifying neighborhoods by their relative conditions and their current market dynamics can open new frontiers of understanding that were inaccessible through decennial census data.

Comparable time series on computer tape in the same format for different cities can accelerate the understanding of changing neighborhood dynamics. That way hidden patterns can most easily be detected. How things actually work, cause and effect, would begin to emerge from the distractions and white noise currently dominating the urban scene.

Developing an annual data base similar to those the R. L. Polk system already maintains in many cities offers a promising foundation. The existing set of cities that have such directories should be reviewed to determine the suitability of the available data for detecting neighborhood change. Do common indicators emerge? Are the formats in various cities compatible? What level of errors do the various elements typically contain?

As soon as possible the data network should be expanded to more cities. Since the Polk urban statistical data are a by-product of services already paid for by subscribers, they cost comparatively little. What other inexpensive means of obtaining complete annual compilations by dwelling unit are possible? Can data on two wage earner households be factored in? Data on race or ethnicity? The system must remain basic and reliable.

Such data must be reviewed in their metropolitan context. In regions where persistent strong housing demand is revealed, policymakers should focus on facilitating production (or reducing household growth) to avoid becoming too preoccupied with its market symptoms of displacement, condominium conversions, and speculation. In areas where demand is slack, planners could then foresee whether the imbalance was likely to remain chronic and thereby reach more creative dispositions for surplus housing.

New theories on urban dynamics will emerge from this improved data base as in any other science. On the one hand this will fine tune the understanding of needs and priorities, on the other it can lead to the specification of more effective interventions. General budget tightening will preclude the continuation of past hit-or-miss strategies even as interest groups become more strident in their demands. Local policymakers will need both the understanding and the more effective interventions to help them deal with these new pressures. The following questions will point them in the right direction:

Are demand and supply roughly in balance overall or are there serious mismatches? If there are, how can the situation be improved? Are housing benefits and costs for all interests open and predictable as the Housing Policy Law states, or are they in fact becoming more and more obscured by public interventions? Are urban property values easy to appraise? Is the private sector developing more conventional housing and rehabilitation? Is there any arson? Are promising partnerships among community, public, and private interests flourishing or are they getting co-opted or dominated by any one interest? What are the functions best handled by the public sector? The private sector? What should be the roles and responsibilities of community residents?

If the planner feels alone in starting on this new course, the following guidelines will prove useful in the interim until better theory and practices are developed:

- View all outside revitalization programs skeptically, including those from Washington. Especially resist copying or seeking programs simply because they are fashionable.

- Proceed to intervene only when you and the various interests have defined *jointly* what is needed.

- Examine ways to improve staff accountability to the public.

- Build the administrative staff into a mutually supportive team.

- Reorganize only where the restructuring naturally emerges from following the above guidelines.

- Seek out and attend workshops that sensitize participants to neighborhood dynamics and to the tactics used by conflicting interests to gain advantage.

- Improvise in monitoring local change along the lines suggested in these chapters. This will enable you to identify what is happening and to judge the effectiveness of interventions.

Experience in several cities already testifies that once the will to pursue such new approaches surfaces, the paths reveal themselves. The changing demographic and fiscal realities will soon force the issue upon many more. There are ample compensations for effectively responding to the coming trauma of change. The rewards of creating a more competent, responsive administration will be that useful, cost saving ideas begin to flow from the citizens. Indeed, the public, private, and community partnership long sought in rhetoric could actually emerge in many cities. As each interest contributes time and resources toward improving homes and neighborhoods in mutual efforts, planners will become more effective and neighborhood revitalization will seem to gather a tailwind.

Bibliography

Ahlbrandt, Roger S.; M.K. Charny; and J.V. Cunningham. 1977. "Citizen Perceptions of Their Neighborhoods." *Journal of Housing* 34, no. 7 (July): 338–41.

Allman, T.D. 1978. "The Urban Crisis Leaves Town." *Harpers* (December): 41–56.

Alonso, William. 1977. "The Population Factor and Urban Structure." Cambridge, Mass.: Harvard University, Center for Population Studies. Working Paper #102 (August).

Anderson, Jervis. 1977. "Reporter at Large: The Making of Boerum Hill." *The New Yorker* (November 14):

Berry, Wendell. 1978. *The Unsettling of America: Culture and Agriculture.* New York: Avon.

Beshers, James M. 1962. *Urban Social Structure.* New York: The Free Press of Glencoe.

Black, J. Thomas. 1975. "Private Market Housing Renovation in Central Cities: a U.L.I. Survey." *Urban Land* (November): 3–9.

Blaine, Edward. 1973. "The Community Improvement Program in Jamaica Plain." Unpublished thesis, Boston University.

Birch, David L. et al. 1977. "The Community Analysis Model: An Overview." Cambridge, Mass.: Joint Center for Urban Studies of the MIT and Harvard University.

Boston Redevelopment Authority and Boston Urban Observatory. 1975. "Working Class Housing: A Study of Triple Deckers in Boston" (May).

Boston Redevelopment Authority and Boston Urban Observatory. 1973. "Subsidized Multifamily Rental Housing in the Boston Metropolitan Area: Analysis and Prognosis" (October).

Boyer, Brian D. 1973. *Cities Destroyed for Cash; the FHA Scandal at HUD.* Chicago: Follett.

Clay, Philip L. 1978a. *Neighborhood Revitalization: Issues, Trends, and Strategies.* Washington: National Endowment for the Arts.

Clay, Philip L. 1978b. "Neighborhood Revitalization and Community Development: The Experience and the Promise." *Center for Community Economic Development Newsletter* (August–October): 1–9.

Downie, Leonard Jr. 1974. *Mortgage on America.* New York: Praeger.

Downs, Anthony and J. Leanne Lachman. 1977. "The Role of Neighborhoods in the Mature Metropolis." Paper prepared for Symposium on Challenges and Opportunities in the Mature Metropolis, St. Louis, Missouri, June 6–8.

Embry, Robert. 1977. "Urban Reinvestment and the Effects of Displacement of Low and Moderate Income Persons." Testimony before the Senate Committee on Banking, Housing, and Urban Affairs, July 7.

Fichter, Robert. 1977. "Young Professionals and City Neighborhoods." Boston, Mass.: Parkman Center for Urban Affairs (August).

Gale, Dennis E. 1977. "The Back-to-the-City Movement . . . or Is It?: A Survey of Recent Homeowners in the Mount Pleasant Neighborhood of Washington, D.C." Washington, D.C.: George Washington University, Department of Urban and Regional Planning.

Garreau, Joel R. 1979. "The Nine Nations of North America." *The Washington Post* (March 4): C 1, 4.

Goetze, Rolf. 1976. *Building Neighborhood Confidence: A Humanistic Strategy for Urban Housing.* Cambridge, Mass.: Ballinger Publishing Company.

Goetze, Rolf; Kent W. Colton; and Vincent F. O'Donnell. 1977. "Stabilizing Neighborhoods: A Fresh Approach to Housing Dynamics and Perceptions." Prepared for HUD, Office of Policy Development and Research, Boston Redevelopment Authority and Public Systems Evaluation, Inc. (November).

Goetze, Rolf. 1978. "Avoiding Both Disinvestment and Speculation in Private Multifamily Housing." *Journal of the American Real Estate and Urban Economics Association* 6, no. 2 (Summer): 175–85.

Grier, George and Eunice Grier. 1978. "Urban Displacement: A Reconnaissance." Memo report prepared for the U.S. Department of Housing and Urban Development (March).

Grier, George and Eunice Grier. 1977. "Movers to the City: New Data on the Housing Market for Washington, D.C." Washington, D.C.: Washington Center for Metropolitan Studies (May).

Holman, Carl. 1977. "Neighborhood Revitalization and Dislocation." Testimony before the Senate Committee on Banking, Housing, and Urban Affairs, July 8.

James, Franklin J. 1977. "Back to the City: An Appraisal of Housing Reinvestment and Population Change in Urban America." Washington, D.C.: The Urban Institute (December).

Kollias, Karen, with Arthur Naparstek and Chester Haskell. 1977. *Neighborhood Reinvestment: A Citizen's Compendium for Programs and Strategies.* Washington, D.C.: National Center for Urban Ethnic Affairs.

Kotler, Milton. 1977. "Dislocation of Long Time Residents Caused by the Growing Pace of Neighborhood Revitalization in Many of Our Older Cities." Testimony before the Senate Committee on Banking, Housing, and Urban Affairs, July 8.

Leven, Charles L., ed. 1978. *The Mature Metropolis*. Lexington, Mass.: D.C. Heath.

Lipton, Gregory. 1977. "Evidence of Central City Revival." *Journal of the American Institute of Planners* 43 (April): 136—47.

Lorenz, Konrad Z. 1973. "The Fashionable Fallacy of Dispensing with Description." *Naturwissenschaften* 60 (January): 1—9.

Massachusetts Arson Prevention Task Force. 1978. Draft report. Office of Lieutenant Governor Thomas P. O'Neill, III. December.

Myers, Phyllis and Gordon Binder. 1977. *Neighborhood Conservation: Lessons from Three Cities, An Issue Report*. Washington, D.C.: The Conservation Foundation.

Naparstek, Arthur J. and Gale Cincotta. 1976. "Urban Disinvestment: New Implications for Community Organization, Research and Public Policy." Washington, D.C.: National Center for Urban Ethnic Affairs and Chicago: National Training and Information Center (February).

The National Urban Coalition. 1978. *Displacement: City Neighborhoods in Transition*. Washington, D.C.

Pattison, Timothy. 1977. "The Process of Neighborhood Upgrading and Gentrification; an Examination of Two Neighborhoods in the Boston Area." Unpublished Master's Thesis, Massachusetts Institute of Technology, Department of City Planning.

Peirce, Neal R. 1977. "Nation's Cities Poised for a Stunning Comeback." *The Washington Post* (July 3).

R.L. Polk and Company. undated. "The T.E.A.M. Approach." *Update: Profiles of Change* no. 8.

Reinhold, Robert. 1977. "Middle-Class Return Displaces Some Urban Poor." *The New York Times* (June 5): 1.

Rogg, Nathaniel H. 1977. "Urban Housing Rehabilitation in the United States." Washington, D.C.: United States League of Savings Associations (December).

Rugo, Robert. 1979. Draft Final Report in Preparation. "Living in Boston: An Innovative Project of Public Information and Promotional Strategies in Support of Neighborhood Preservation." City of Boston, Office of Program Development, Boston, Mass.

Schur, Robert and Virginia Sherry. 1977. "The Neighborhood Housing Movement." New York: Association of Neighborhood Housing Developers.

Spears, John P. 1978. "Changes in Housing Conditions in Jamaica Plain, 1974—1978." Unpublished data, Boston Architectual Center.

SRI International. 1978. "Jarvis, U.S.A." Menlo Park, California: Center for Urban and Regional Planning (June).

SRI International. 1979. "Using New Governance Tools to Solve Local Government Problems." Menlo Park, California: Center for Urban and Regional Planning (January).

Stanfield, Rochelle L. 1976. "Cities Being Rehabilitated, though Housing Ills Remain." *National Journal* (July 17): 1004—9.

Turner, John F.C. 1977. *Housing by People; Towards Autonomy in Building Environments*. New York: Pantheon Books.

UHAB, 1977. "The Urban Homesteading Assistance Board: Third Annual Progress Report." New York: Cathedral House.

U.S. Department of Housing and Urban Development, Office of Policy Development and Research. 1975. *The Dynamics of Neighborhood Change.* San Francisco: Public Affairs Counseling.

U.S. House of Representatives, Committee on Banking, Currency, and Housing. 1976. Hearings "The Rebirth of the American City." Washington, D.C. September 20—October 1.

U.S. Senate, Committee on Banking, Housing, and Urban Affairs. 1977. Hearings "Neighborhood Diversity, Problems of Dislocation and Diversity in Communities Undergoing Neighborhood Revitalization Activity." Washington, D.C. 95th 1st session, July 7 and 8.

Urban Consortium. 1977. "The Displacement Problem in Revitalized Urban Neighborhoods." Washington, D.C.: Report of the Community and Economic Development Task Force (September).

Warren, Rachelle and Donald I. Warren. 1977. *The Neighborhood Organizer's Handbook.* Notre Dame: University of Notre Dame Press.

Weiler, Conrad. 1978. "Reinvestment Displacement: HUD's Role in a New Housing Issue." Washington, D.C.: Paper prepared for the Office of Community Planning and Development, U.S. Department of Housing and Urban Development (January).

Weiler, Conrad. 1977. "Urban Reinvestment and Its Effects on Displacement of Low- and Moderate-Income Residents." Washington, D.C.: Testimony before Senate Committee on Banking, Housing, and Urban Affairs, July 8.

Whiteside, William. 1977. "Dislocation of Poor and Minorities Caused by Neighborhood Revitalization in Older Cities." Washington, D.C.: Testimony before Senate Committee on Banking, Housing, and Urban Affairs, July 8.

Yin, Robert K. et al. 1978. "Federal Aid and Urban Economic Development: A Local Perspective." Draft report. Santa Monica, California: The Rand Corporation.

Index

About the Author

Since 1968, **Rolf Goetze** has been a neighborhood watcher, intimately involved with the design and evaluation of urban housing programs.

After receiving a master's degree in architecture from Harvard University in 1962, he and his wife served with the Peace Corps in Nepal where they learned first hand how people with limited resources can be given the assistance they need to help themselves. Upon their return to the United States, Rolf Goetze became involved in domestic community development and completed a Ph.D. in housing and social policy analysis at Massachusetts Institute of Technology.

Dr. Goetze is presently director of housing and revitalization programs for the Boston Redevelopment Authority. He lives in neighboring Belmont with his wife and four children. He also lectures widely and is currently participating in a national study of local neighborhood assistance practices.